Elizabeth Cartwright, PhD
Pascale Allotey, PhD
Editors

Women's Health: New Frontiers in Advocacy & Social Justice Research

Women's Health: New Frontiers in Advocacy & Social Justice Research has been co-published simultaneously as *Women & Health*, Volume 43, Number 4 2006.

Pre-publication
REVIEWS,
COMMENTARIES,
EVALUATIONS . . .

"CHALLENGES THOSE WHO PRACTICE COMMUNITY-BASED PARTICIPATORY RESEARCH (CBPR) to examine their role and obligation as advocates. Cartwright and Allotey defy the conservative pressures of our scientific community which views advocacy work as subjective, morally driven, and evidence-weak. The authors in this volume suggest, instead, that direct links exist between sound CBPR methods and informed advocacy. Readers will appreciate the extremely complex cross-cultural dilemmas laid bare here, for example: a woman's grief and horror when medical staff delay the delivery of her dead fetus from her body because of the genital cutting she experienced decades prior; or the incongruous policy of a domestic violence shelter that denies services to women's sons older than twelve, on the legalistic precedent that assumes these boys are most likely a batterer or sexual perpetrator. In direct and compelling language, the authors call for advocacy by researchers who discover such social injustices. Importantly, this volume also offers some initial models, ranging from lay advocacy to lobbying and education efforts by researchers. Cartwright and Allotey remind us that advocacy is not only an important response to inequity and marginalization, it is what our informants expect of us."

Carolyn Smith-Morris, PhD, MS
Assistant Professor
Southern Methodist University (SMU)
Department of Anthropology
Chair
Council on Anthropology & Reproduction
Society for Medical Anthropology

More pre-publication
REVIEWS, COMMENTARIES, EVALUATIONS . . .

"In this THOUGHT-PROVOKING collection of essays the authors use their research in women's health to draw attention to important questions about research and advocacy in social science. . . . The research settings and health issues in the articles range widely. The authors in the collection embrace the community-based, participatory research model in varying degrees and with varying success. Rather than detracting from the effectiveness of the volume's goals, these variations serves to demonstrate the flexibility and some of the limitations of the model. Cartwright and Allotey have opened an important dialogue with this volume. For readers who are teetering on the brink of advocacy in their own research agendas, this is A VALUABLE COLLECTION. It is also a collection that will be useful in research method, research design and community-based research and service-learning (CBRSL) courses for students in anthropology, sociology and especially those whose interests cross disciplinary divides with medicine, nursing or public health."

Carolyn Behrman, PhD
Associate Professor of Anthropology
University of Akron

"Cartwright and Allotey have created A SPLENDID RESOURCE FOR RESEARCHERS, EDUCATORS, AND ADVOCATES interested in going beyond the traditional research methodologies when interested in social problems affecting marginalized populations. In the context of growing inequality in the United States and in the world and an expanded knowledge base on health disparities and faced with the limitations inherent in traditional methods, many researchers are interested in participatory action research because of its democratic and empowering capacities. In this volume, Cartwright and Allotey, offer an array of chapters that demonstrate participatory action research in process investigating health related issues affecting marginalized women. Although all chapters make significant contributions, I found the chapter on assisting refugee women to take control of their reproductive needs and using participatory research to build an effective Type 2 diabetes intervention with female Latin-American farmworkers, PARTICULARLY INNOVATIVE. This book WILL BECOME A SIGNIFICANT REFERENCE POINT as we search for new models of researching and affecting the growing disparities inherent in today's world from a social justice perspective."

Silvia Domínguez, PhD
Sociology and Anthropology
Northeastern University, Boston

More pre-publication
REVIEWS, COMMENTARIES, EVALUATIONS . . .

"An unique collection of papers that demonstrate the importance of intervention efforts when the researcher has taken the role of advocate. . . . SHOULD BE 'UNMISSABLE' READING for those who want to learn more about the successes of community-based participatory action research. Although the specific examples focus on issues around women's health, the interest should be much broader across the interface between social anthropology and public health. The paper on domestic violence will be found THOUGHT-PROVOKING and salutary for those involved in any voluntary sector advocacy setting. . . . The two editors are distinguished researchers in the field and contribute themselves to three of the five main studies described. Examples come from disadvantaged populations in Australia and the USA, covering refugee, Indigenous Women, immigrants and rural communities, with specific studies in domestic violence, cervical cancer, type II diabetes and the use of lay advocates. Work described among and with indigenous women in Queensland, Australia, takes us through the research and advocacy to successful changes in health policy leading to culturally appropriate services, providing ample justification for this approach to research, if it were needed. . . . HIGHLY COMMENDED, AND NOT JUST TO THOSE ALREADY CONVERTED TO THIS RESEARCH APPROACH."

Dr. Hilary Pickles, MA, PhD, FRCP, FFPH
Director of Public Health and Health Strategy
Hillingdon Primary Care Trust
United Kingdom

Women's Health:
New Frontiers
in Advocacy
& Social Justice Research

Women's Health: New Frontiers in Advocacy & Social Justice Research has been co-published simultaneously as *Women & Health*, Volume 43, Number 4 2006.

Monographic Separates from the *Women & Health*™

For additional information on these and other Haworth Press titles, including descriptions, tables of contents, reviews, and prices, use the QuickSearch catalog at http://www.HaworthPress.com.

Women's Health: New Frontiers in Advocacy & Social Justice Research, edited by Elizabeth Cartwright, PhD, and Pascale Allotey, PhD (Vol. 43, No. 4, 2006). *Examines how researchers can become advocates when the marginalization of community groups affects access to the programs and services they need.*

Teaching Gender, Teaching Women's Health: Case Studies in Medical and Health Science Education, edited by Lenore Manderson, PhD, FASSA (Vol. 37, No. 4, 2003). *"VALUABLE to anyone involved in medical and health science education. . . . Provides much-needed insight." (Ursula K. Snyder, PhD, Editor/Program Director, Medscape Ob/Gyn & Women's Health, New York City)*

Environmental, Policy and Cultural Factors Related to Physical Activity in a Diverse Sample of Women: The Women's Cardiovascular Health Network Project, edited by Amy A. Eyler, PhD (Vol. 36, No. 2, 2002). *"INTERESTING AND UNIQUE. . . . A MUST-READ for anyone interested in designing, implementing, and evaluating physical activity interventions for underserved–and typically inactive–women." (Lynda Randsell. PhD, FACSM, Assistant Professor of Exercise & Sport Science, University of Utah-Salt Lake City)*

Women's Health in Mainland Southeast Asia, edited by Andrea Whittaker, PhD (Vol. 35, No. 4, 2002). *Shows how war, military regimes, industrialization, urbanization, and social upheaval have all affected the choices Southeast Asian women make about their health and health care.*

Domestic Violence and Health Care: Policies and Prevention, edited by Carolina Reyes, MD, William J. Rudman, PhD, and Calvin R. Hewitt, MBA (Vol. 35, No. 2/3, 2002). *Examines the role of health care in the struggle to combat domestic violence.*

Women's Work, Health and Quality of Life, edited by Afaf Ibrahim Meleis, PhD, FAAN (Vol. 33, No. 1/2, 2001). *"A FINE COLLECTION. . . . A useful supplement for courses on women and health. It is particularly helpful to have a collection that reports research on women in different countries. . . . Describes role overload, role strain, and stress that occurs when immigrants try to adjust to a new culture." (Eleanor Krassen Covan, PhD, Professor of Sociology, Director of Gerontology, University of North Carolina, Wilmington)*

Welfare, Work and Well-Being, edited by Mary Clare Lennon, PhD, MS (Vol. 32, No. 1/2 & No. 3, 2001). *Examines the relationship between social roles, economic circumstances, material hardship, and child well-being among low-income women.*

Australian Women's Health: Innovations in Social Science and Community Research, edited by Lenore Manderson, PhD (Vol. 28, No. 1, 1998). *Reflects a wider approach to women's health, which moves from maternity and fertility issues to question the impact of gender on all aspects of the disease experience.*

Women, Drug Use and HIV Infection, edited by Sally J. Stevens, PhD, Stephanie Tortu, PhD, and Susan L. Coyle, PhD (Vol. 27, No. 1/2, 1998). *"A much-needed resource of critical information about the largest initiative to date designed to prevent HIV among drug users and their sexual partners." (Robert E. Booth, PhD, Associate Professor of Psychiatry, University of Colorado School of Medicine, Denver)*

Women in the Later Years: Health, Social, and Cultural Perspectives, edited by Lois Grau, PhD, RN, in collaboration with Ida Susser, PhD (Vol. 14, No. 3/4, 1989). *"An excellent overview of the pertinent social, political, and personal issues of this long-ignored group." (News for Women in Psychiatry)*

Government Policy and Women's Health Care: The Swedish Alternative, edited by Gunnela Westlander, PhD, and Jeanne Mager Stellman, PhD (Vol. 13, No. 3/4, 1988). *"An illuminating, comprehensive overview of Swedish women's health and their productive and reproductive roles." (Freda L. Paltiel, Senior Advisor, Status of Women, Health and Welfare Canada, Ottawa, Ontario, Canada)*

Embryos, Ethics, and Women's Rights: Exploring the New Reproductive Technologies, edited by Elaine Hoffman Baruch, Amadeo F. D'Adamo, Jr., and Joni Seager (Vol. 13, No. 1/2, 1988). *"Groundbreaking . . . Reveals the myriad of perspectives from which the new technologies can be regarded. Particularly thought-provoking are discussions that link surrogacy to economic and class issues." (Publishers Weekly)*

Women, Health, and Poverty (also published as Dealing with the Health Needs of Women in Poverty), edited by Cesar A. Perales and Lauren S. Young, EdD (Vol. 12, No. 3/4, 1988). *"Succeeds in alerting readers to many important issues. . . Should be useful to public policymakers, researchers, and others interested in understanding the health problems of poor women." (Contemporary Psychology)*

Women and Cancer, edited by Steven D. Stellman, PhD (Vol. 11, No. 3/4, 1987). *"The contributors succeed in increasing the reader's awareness of cancer in women and in stimulating thought processes in reference to the need for further research." (Oncology Nursing Forum)*

Health Needs of Women as They Age, edited by Sharon Golub, PhD, and Rita Jackaway Freedman, PhD (Vol. 10, No. 2/3, 1985). *"The contributors distill a great deal of general information on aging into an easily readable and understandable format . . . A useful primer." (The New England Journal of Medicine)*

Health Care of the Female Adolescent, edited by Sharon Golub, PhD (Vol. 9, No. 2/3, 1985). *"An excellent collection of well-written and carefully selected articles designed to provide up-to-date information about the health problems of adolescent girls." (Journal of the American Medical Women's Association)*

Lifting the Curse of Menstruation: A Feminist Appraisal of the Influence of Menstruation on Women's Lives, edited by Sharon Golub, PhD (Vol. 8, No. 2/3, 1983). *"Crammed with information and well-documented. Written in a professional style, each chapter is followed by extensive lists of notes and references." (Journal of Sex Education and Therapy)*

Obstetrical Intervention and Technology in the 1980s, edited by Diony Young, BA (Vol. 7, No. 3/4, 1983). *"Every family physician and obstetrician in North America should read this book." (Canadian Family Physician)*

ALL HAWORTH MEDICAL PRESS BOOKS
AND JOURNALS ARE PRINTED
ON CERTIFIED ACID-FREE PAPER

Women's Health: New Frontiers in Advocacy & Social Justice Research

Elizabeth Cartwright, PhD
Pascale Allotey, PhD
Editors

Women's Health: New Frontiers in Advocacy & Social Justice Research has been co-published simultaneously as *Women & Health*, Volume 43, Number 4 2006.

The Haworth Medical Press®
An Imprint of The Haworth Press, Inc.

New York • London • Victoria (AU)
www.HaworthPress.com

Published by

The Haworth Medical Press®, 10 Alice Street, Binghamton, NY 13904-1580 USA

The Haworth Medical Press® is an imprint of The Haworth Press, Inc., 10 Alice Street, Binghamton, NY 13904-1580 USA.

Women's Health: New Frontiers in Advocacy & Social Justice Research has been co-published simultaneously as *Women & Health*, Volume 43, Number 4 2006.

The development, preparation, and publication of this work has been undertaken with great care. However, the publisher, employees, editors, and agents of The Haworth Press and all imprints of The Haworth Press, Inc., including The Haworth Medical Press® and Pharmaceutical Products Press®, are not responsible for any errors contained herein or for consequences that may ensue from use of materials or information contained in this work. With regard to case studies, identities and circumstances of individuals discussed herein have been changed to protect confidentiality. Any resemblance to actual persons, living or dead, is entirely coincidental.

The Haworth Press is committed to the dissemination of ideas and information according to the highest standards of intellectual freedom and the free exchange of ideas. Statements made and opinions expressed in this publication do not necessarily reflect the views of the Publisher, Directors, management, or staff of The Haworth Press, Inc., or an endorsement by them.

Library of Congress Cataloging-in-Publication Data

Women's health : new frontiers in advocacy & social justice research / Elizabeth Cartwright, Pascale Allotey, editors.
     p. ; cm.
     "Co-published simultaneously as Women & health, volume 43, number 4."
     Includes bibliographical references and index.
     ISBN-13: 978-0-7890-3330-7 (hard cover : alk. paper)
     ISBN-10: 0-7890-3330-5 (hard cover : alk. paper)
     ISBN-13: 978-0-7890-3331-4 (soft cover : alk. paper)
     ISBN-10: 0-7890-3331-3 (soft cover : alk. paper)
     1. Women's health services. 2. Patient advocacy. I. Cartwright, Elizabeth, 1959- . II. Allotey, Pascale.
     [DNLM: 1. Women's Health. 2. Patient Advocacy. 3. Social Justice. 4. Women's Health Services. W1 WO478 v.43 no. 4 2006 / WA 309 W9737 2006]
     RA564.85W682 2006
     362.1082–dc22

                             2006020040

Indexing, Abstracting & Website/Internet Coverage

This section provides you with a list of major indexing & abstracting services and other tools for bibliographic access. That is to say, each service began covering this periodical during the year noted in the right column. Most Websites which are listed below have indicated that they will either post, disseminate, compile, archive, cite or alert their own Website users with research-based content from this work. (This list is as current as the copyright date of this publication.)

Abstracting, Website/Indexing Coverage . . . . Year When Coverage Began

- *(CAB ABSTRACTS, CABI) Available in print, diskettes updated weekly, and on INTERNET. Providing full bibliographic listings, author affiliation, augmented keyword searching.* <http://www.cabi.org/> **1992**

- *(IBR) International Bibliography of Book Reviews on the Humanities and Social Sciences (Thomson)* <http://www.saur.de> **2006**

- *(IBZ) International Bibliography of Periodical Literature on the Humanities and Social Sciences (Thomson)* <http://www.saur.de> . . **1996**

- *Abstracts in Anthropology* <http://www.baywood.com/Journals/ PreviewJournals.asp?Id=0001-3455> **1991**

- *Abstracts on Hygiene and Communicable Diseases (CAB ABSTRACTS, CABI)* <http://www.cabi.org> **1992**

- *Academic ASAP (Thomson Gale)* **1988**

- *Academic Search Premier (EBSCO)* <http://www.epnet.com/academic/acasearchprem.asp> **1993**

- *Biological Sciences Database (Cambridge Scientific Abstracts)* <http://www.csa.com> **2006**

- *Biology Digest (in print & online)* <http://www.infotoday.com> **1991**

- *Cambridge Scientific Abstracts (A leading publisher of scientific information in print journals, online databases, CD-ROM and via the Internet)* <http://www.csa.com> **2006**

(continued)

(continued)

(continued)

(continued)

(continued)

Special Bibliographic Notes related to special journal issues (separates) and indexing/abstracting:

- indexing/abstracting services in this list will also cover material in any "separate" that is co-published simultaneously with Haworth's special thematic journal issue or DocuSerial. Indexing/abstracting usually covers material at the article/chapter level.
- monographic co-editions are intended for either non-subscribers or libraries which intend to purchase a second copy for their circulating collections.
- monographic co-editions are reported to all jobbers/wholesalers/approval plans. The source journal is listed as the "series" to assist the prevention of duplicate purchasing in the same manner utilized for books-in-series.
- to facilitate user/access services all indexing/abstracting services are encouraged to utilize the co-indexing entry note indicated at the bottom of the first page of each article/chapter/contribution.
- this is intended to assist a library user of any reference tool (whether print, electronic, online, or CD-ROM) to locate the monographic version if the library has purchased this version but not a subscription to the source journal.
- individual articles/chapters in any Haworth publication are also available through the Haworth Document Delivery Service (HDDS).

Women's Health: New Frontiers in Advocacy & Social Justice Research

CONTENTS

ABOUT THE EDITORS

Elizabeth Cartwright, PhD, is an Associate Professor of Anthropology and Director of the Hispanic Health Projects at Idaho State University, Pocatello, Idaho. Dr. Cartwright's background is in medical anthropology and nursing. She has many years of experience working in community based participatory research and education projects both in the U.S. and in Latin America. Her research has focused on migration and health, women's health and environmental health issues.

Pascale Allotey, PhD, is currently the Chair of Race and Diversity at the School of Health Sciences and Social Care, and Centre for Public Health Research at Brunel University, West London. She has a background in epidemiology and medical anthropology. Her research has focused on the health of marginalized populations and she has published extensively on gender and tropical diseases, disability in developing countries, reproductive health and rights and the health of refugees and asylum seekers.

Women's Health:
New Frontiers in Advocacy
& Social Justice Research–
Introduction

Elizabeth Cartwright, PhD
Pascale Allotey, PhD

Public health research and practice today faces many new challenges. Major threats to human security have occurred, including: natural disasters from tsunamis, hurricanes and earthquakes; violent deaths from civil unrest and population displacement; terrorism; new, emerging and continuing pandemics ranging from HIV/AIDS to Avian influenza; and persistent and chronic disease from worsening poverty and social inequalities. These challenges create and sustain vulnerabilities that require new and innovative interventions, which take account of the importance of the power differentials between the vulnerable and marginalized populations most affected by these threats. The challenges also require the expertise and efforts of researchers, practitioners and policy-makers whose role it is to explore and address these issues. Recent events, such as the catastrophic hurricanes along the Gulf coast of the United States brought into stark reality the non-randomness of the

Elizabeth Cartwright is Associate Professor of Anthropology and Director of the Hispanic Health Projects, Idaho State University, Pocatello, Idaho. Pascale Allotey is Chair of Race and Diversity, School of Health Sciences and Social Care, and Centre for Public Health Research, Brunel University, West London.

[Haworth co-indexing entry note]: "Women's Health: New Frontiers in Advocacy & Social Justice Research–Introduction." Cartwright, Elizabeth, and Pascale Allotey. Co-published simultaneously in *Women & Health* (The Haworth Medical Press, an imprint of The Haworth Press, Inc.) Vol. 43, No. 4, 2006, pp. 1-6; and: *Women's Health: New Frontiers in Advocacy & Social Justice Research* (ed: Elizabeth Cartwright, and Pascale Allotey) The Haworth Medical Press, an imprint of The Haworth Press, Inc., 2006, pp. 1-6. Single or multiple copies of this article are available for a fee from The Haworth Document Delivery Service [1-800-HAWORTH, 9:00 a.m. - 5:00 p.m. (EST). E-mail address: docdelivery@haworthpress.com].

Available online at http://wh.haworthpress.com
doi:10.1300/J013v43n04_01

distribution of disadvantage and the persistence of vulnerable sectors of U.S. communities. They also highlighted the lack of evidence on the most effective ways of working with marginalized communities to optimize the effectiveness of health interventions.

Traditional research paradigms that employ the structured research tools offered in epidemiology, controlled trials and other intervention research may be ineffective in responding to dynamic social, cultural and environmental contexts. In part, these approaches reflect investigator-driven research priorities. In addition the study designs require "control" of factors considered external to the variables of interest that may otherwise compromise the interpretation of data. Without discounting the merits of this type of evidence, clear difficulties arise in integrating interventions that are designed on the basis of evidence obtained under structured and controlled conditions, into the realities of daily existence of communities that face persistent vulnerabilities.

In these instances, advocacy plays a critical role in attempting to address social injustice in situations of vulnerability. Advocates represent those unable to represent themselves. However, a major part of public health discourse discounts the importance of advocacy because of the strong moral underpinnings, subjective nature of the process and perceived weakness of its evidence base (Murray 1996, Murray 1997). In addition, in circumstances in which advocacy has led the development of interventions, the evidence base for monitoring and evaluation of these efforts is at best, very thin. Research approaches are, therefore, needed that are flexible and responsive to changing demographics and increasing vulnerabilities, and that allow for advocacy where appropriate but without compromising the rigor and robustness of the methods or the reliability and validity of the findings. Such approaches are possible through combining phenomenological approaches from anthropology with the underlying principles and positivist approaches embodied in more conventional public health research.

In this collection, we have brought together a unique selection of papers that demonstrate the importance of and outcomes of intervention efforts when the researcher has taken the role of advocate and the use of community-based participatory action research. The health issues addressed in these efforts are as varied as the range of backgrounds of investigators and communities with whom research was conducted. The common theme across the varied efforts described in the papers in this volume was marginalization of community groups. For most, the lack of power and the extent of their marginalization hindered their access to the relevant services and programs that would address their needs. The studies were based in Australia, New Zealand and the US, and the communities included resettling refugee women, rural women and Indigenous women in Australia and New Zealand and Hispanic migrant women and victims of domestic violence in the U.S. The health issues addressed include cancer, domestic violence and diabetes.

COMMUNITY BASED PARTICIPATORY RESEARCH (CBPR): MOVING THE PARADIGM INTO THE FUTURE

Collaboration between academics and community partners is a complex process. McAllister et al. (2003), describe the growing acceptance of community-based participatory research (CBPR) among public health researchers and began to evaluate the meaning of the term *collaboration*. These authors conceptualized collaboration as a relationship facilitated by hiring community members at the onset of a research project and by promoting an atmosphere of teamwork throughout the project's conceptualization, data gathering, analysis, and dissemination of results back to the community. Eliciting community members' opinions and perspectives throughout the research process allows researchers to refine their questions and approaches as the research project progresses. McAllister et al. (2003, p. 1673) concluded that to be effective, community-based research should be based on:

1. Collaboration between researchers and community-based partners in determining the research focus and design,
2. Community-focused recruitment of research participants,
3. Full use of the expertise of community-based research staff,
4. Shared oversight of the research process, and
5. Sharing of preliminary findings with community partners and incorporation of their interpretations in reporting findings and conducting further analyses.

The papers in this volume describe different levels of community participation in the research process. Each paper describes an implementation of the CBPR model that is uniquely tailored to the research questions and needs of the particular study community. The refugee women in New Zealand and Australia negotiated changes in a researcher-driven project and thereafter, took an active role the evolution of the project (Guerin, Allotey et al.). The rural Australian women had full control of their program of support, and the role of the researcher was largely as an observer to their advocacy development (Warren, Markovic et al.). An anthropologist-advocate was invited by the director of a domestic violence program to engage in long-term ethnography and to describe critically the social processes at work among victims of domestic violence, their children and the professionals who try to ameliorate this difficult situation (Schow). The Indigenous women in Australia initiated the project on cancer and invited the researchers to support and work with them on what was for them, a health priority (Manderson and Hoban). Hispanic women and researchers worked together in the rural Western U.S. for five years studying the problem of type 2 diabetes, educating the community as a whole about the health effects of this disease and advocating for access to appropriate health education and medical care for those who suffer from this disease (Cartwright et al.). The common theme that runs through these articles is the expressed need of women in the communities to avoid the sanitization or minimization of the many variables present in their life situations that are integral to their experiences of ill-health. The roles of the researchers as advocates and the effects of this role on the research findings are also explored.

Taken as a whole, these papers demonstrate that CBPR is a flexible paradigm within which scientifically rigorous research can be conducted while attending to the felt needs of the community members. Anthropologist Merrill Singer conceptualizes advocacy on a continuum from purely knowledge-oriented advocacy that includes teaching and writing in a manner that promotes human understanding and demands an acknowledgement of the suffering of oppressed group, to a more action-oriented advocacy in which the anthropologist promotes the specific interest of a subordinate group (Singer 1990, p. 549). Explicit and critical witnessing and writing along with finely tuned CBPR work provides the conceptual and ideological groundwork of the approaches used in this volume.

ADVOCACY AND SOCIAL SCIENCE: EVOLVING CONSIDERATIONS

CBPR as a research strategy is not a static approach; as community members gain knowledge and control over research methods and the use of data, existing hierarchies of power within health research will change. As social scientists work alongside community members, not only are research results shared with the community, but the community members themselves also can engage in the process of education and professional development that will allow them to become full members of the community-based research teams. The papers in this volume describe communities at different levels of knowledge about and use of CBPR. Control over the implementation of the projects and dissemination of results varied between projects and over time within the same research projects. For instance, in the Hispanic communities focusing on the study of type 2 diabetes, community members were first involved as bilingual interviewers, then became permanent members of the on-going research projects housed at a local university (Cartwright et al.) and currently, several of these individuals are enrolled as undergraduate and graduate students who are actively creating their own expertise in health research. Understanding the evolution of power over time in CBPR research is a topic for future research consideration.

Another topic for future research is a more refined understanding of the effects of the proliferation of new communicative technologies on CBPR. Cell phones, video cameras, and personal computers are changing patterns of access to information and to real-time knowledge of events on a worldwide basis. Individuals living in remote regions are now often capable of communicating directly with the larger world without the need for academic or other intermediaries. What will be the ramifications of these changes for social scientists whose research focuses on community health and disaster planning or on the more urgent needs of individuals living in vulnerable situations such as refugee camps or other kinds of temporary accommodations? The processes of advocacy and community-based research on public health issues will need to evolve along with these changing social realities. The papers in this volume illustrate that sound scientific research can be carried out while advocating for social justice with respect to chronic and emergent health problems in a variety of cultural and regional settings.

REFERENCES

McAllister, C. L. et al. (2003). Parents, Practitioners, and Researchers: Community-Based Participatory Research with Early Head Start. *American Journal of Public Health* 93(10). 1672-1679.

Murray, C. J. L. (1996). Rethinking DALYs. In C. J. L. Murray & A. D. Lopez (Eds.), The global burden of disease: A comprehensive assessment of mortality and disability from diseases, injuries, and risk factors in 1990 and projected to 2020 (pp. 1-98). Cambridge, MA: Harvard School of Public Health.

Murray, C. J. L., & Acharya, A. K. (1997). Understanding DALYs. *Journal of Health Economics, 16*(6), 703-730.

Singer, M. (1990). Another Perspective on Advocacy. *Current Anthropology 31*(5). 548-550.

doi:10.1300/J013v43n04_01

Advocacy as a Means to an End: Assisting Refugee Women to Take Control of Their Reproductive Health Needs

Pauline B. Guerin, PhD
Pascale Allotey, PhD
Fatuma Hussein Elmi, BSN, RN
Samia Baho, MWH

Pauline B. Guerin is affiliated with the School of Psychology, Magill Campus, University of South Australia. At the time that this work was completed she was Senior Research Fellow, Psychology Department and Migration Research Group, University of Waikato, New Zealand. Pascale Allotey is Chair of Race and Diversity, School of Health Sciences and Social Care, Brunel University, West London. Fatuma Hussein Elmi is Research Officer, Psychology Department and Migration Research Group, University of Waikato, Private Bag 3105, Hamilton, New Zealand (E-mail: elmif@hotmail.com). Samia Baho is Research Officer, Key Centre for Women's Health, School of Population Health, University of Melbourne, Victoria 3010, Australia (E-mail: samiabaho@hotmail.com).

Address correspondence to: Pauline B. Guerin, PhD, School of Psychology, Magill Campus, University South Australia, Magill, 5072, Adelaide, Australia (E-mail: Pauline.guerin@unisa.edu.au).

The authors would like to acknowledge the members of the community advisory group of the Australian study, women from the communities who participated in the study and staff of the hospitals and agencies who were open to implementing changes on the basis of the data. They would also like to thank Professor Lenore Manderson for her enduring guidance and support over the duration of the study. The original study was funded by the National Health and Medical Research Council of Australia and parts were conducted under a public health research fellowship from the Victorian Health Promotion Foundation. For the New Zealand study, the authors would like to thank all of the women who participated in the study and Professor Bernard Guerin for helpful comments on drafts of this document and ongoing advice and support for the research.

[Haworth co-indexing entry note]: "Advocacy as a Means to an End: Assisting Refugee Women to Take Control of Their Reproductive Health Needs." Guerin, Pauline B. et al. Co-published simultaneously in *Women & Health* (The Haworth Medical Press, an imprint of The Haworth Press, Inc.) Vol. 43, No. 4, 2006, pp. 7-25; and: *Women's Health: New Frontiers in Advocacy & Social Justice Research* (ed: Elizabeth Cartwright, and Pascale Allotey) The Haworth Medical Press, an imprint of The Haworth Press, Inc., 2006, pp. 7-25. Single or multiple copies of this article are available for a fee from The Haworth Document Delivery Service [1-800-HAWORTH, 9:00 a.m. - 5:00 p.m. (EST). E-mail address: docdelivery@haworthpress.com].

SUMMARY. Negotiating reproductive rights is particularly complex for resettling migrant women from refugee backgrounds. In our ongoing work with women who have fled from countries in Africa and the Middle East, and have resettled in Australia and New Zealand, subtleties of discrimination and perceptions of human rights discriminations were revealed through the complex interplay between research and advocacy. Community Based Participatory Research (CBPR) has therefore been critical in assisting women to identify their needs and negotiate acceptable solutions with health services. This paper presents qualitative and quantitative findings of research with women from refugee backgrounds in Australia (n = 255) and New Zealand (n = 64). The research questions were a combination of community-driven and researcher initiated issues and the projects developed through a continuous iterative process involving feedback from women in the community. We highlight the essential role of advocacy in CBPR and how that can enhance research quality. We argue for the justification of this approach as not only valid and credible but essential in research with these and other communities. doi:10.1300/J013v43n04_02 *[Article copies available for a fee from The Haworth Document Delivery Service: 1-800-HAWORTH. E-mail address: <docdelivery@haworthpress.com> Website: <http://www.HaworthPress.com> © 2006 by The Haworth Press, Inc. All rights reserved.]*

KEYWORDS. Refugee, women, reproductive health, community-based participatory research, advocacy

The events that lead to displacement, such as complex humanitarian emergencies, result in the loss of stability and cultural and social infrastructure. Displaced persons often deal with corrupt bureaucracies, have difficulties in securing the basic needs of food, shelter and health care and experience fear and anxiety over uncertainties about the future. Many of these experiences result in the erosion of trust, particularly of those in authority (Daniel & Knusden, 1995).

The early 1980s saw an increasing awareness of the gendered nature of the refugee experience (Barnett, 2002; Callamard, 1999). The safety of many refugee women and girls was difficult to ensure against violence, rape and other forms of exploitation, particularly in the absence of the traditional support and protection of male family members. The women-at-risk program was created to give priority to the resettlement of refugee women in this category who have been identified by the United Nations High Commissioner for Refugees (UNHCR). The governments of Australia and New Zealand set a quota of 10% of refugee intake for women-at-risk (Manderson, Kelaher, Markovic, & McManus, 1998; NZIS, 2004). However, resettlement, particularly of refugees from low-income countries in Africa, Asia and the Middle East (and to a lesser extent, Eastern Europe), presents challenges due to a wider cultural chasm that impedes successful integration. Lack of language proficiency has been identified as the primary barrier (Beiser & Feng, 2001). Other studies have identified difficulties in understanding the health, education and welfare systems (Manderson & Allotey, 2003a, 2003b) as well as technologies and environmental conditions often taken for granted by the host populations (Guerin, Guerin, Diiriye, & Abdi, 2004; Guerin, Diiriye, Corrigan, & Guerin, 2003).

Of the 9.7 million refugees worldwide at the end of 2003, less than 60,000 were resettled in 10 high-income countries, including 11,860 to Australia and 650 to New Zealand (UNHCR, 2005). Their countries of origin included Afghanistan, Sudan, Burundi, the Democratic Republic of Congo, Palestine, Somalia, Iraq, Viet Nam, Liberia and Angola. In accepting these humanitarian settlers, host countries took on the obligation to assist in their resettlement and integration into their new home.

This paper focuses on the experiences of resettling refugee women from Horn of African and Middle Eastern countries in Australia and New Zealand. Concerns were raised by resettlement support services in health, welfare and education of the needs of these "new and emerging" communities because of their considerable cultural and linguistic diversity. Within the health services, one of the main concerns was the cultural practice of female genital cutting (FGC)[1] prevalent in some of the countries of origin in these communities. As a result, much of the research on women from these communities has focused on reproductive complications associated with FGC (Allotey, Manderson, & Grover, 2001; Knight, Hotchin, Bayly, & Grover, 1999). However, in the course of conducting research with the communities, refugee women[2] became proactive partners in the research process, identifying areas that presented priorities for them. They worked with researchers to highlight relevant research questions for which they required advocacy. This process was critical particularly in the light of previous experiences of betrayed trust relationships (Verdirame, Harrell-Bond, Lomo, & Garry, 2005).

This paper provides a critical examination of how two independent groups of social scientists, committed to the philosophy of advocacy, researched the experiences of resettling refugee women from Horn of African and Middle Eastern countries in Australia and New Zealand. New data are presented from both research projects and discussed in the light of Community-Based Participatory Research (CBPR) and advocacy issues in a manner that refines current understandings of this research methodology. The aim of the Australian study was to enhance the understanding of the immigration experience on the reproductive health of women from Horn of African and Middle Eastern countries resident in Victoria[3] (Allotey, Manderson, Baho, & Demian, 2004). The aim of the New Zealand study was to provide a safe means by which Somali women could express their views about FGC (Guerin & Elmi, 2004, 2005). Our analysis of these two CBPR projects shows that the negotiation and prioritization of research topics informs our understanding of the process of CBPR and advocacy.

STUDY 1: AUSTRALIA

The wave of refugee arrivals in the mid-1990s from countries where FGC is practiced gave impetus to the development of a national program for the elimination of FGC within the target communities. The program prioritized the obstetric and gynecological management of women who had undergone various forms of FGC.

Methods

An ethnographic cohort design was employed with predominantly qualitative methods, using in-depth, open-ended and unstructured interviews, focus group discussions and participant observation. The study was approved by the Human Research Ethics Committee of the University of Melbourne, and informed consent was obtained from all the participants in the study.

Sample. It was difficult to obtain an estimate of the size of the population of refugee women from countries that practice FGC. This was due in part to the mobility of these communities both between states and within Melbourne. Based on available census data the combined estimates of the target population (women between the ages of 20-44 years from Horn of African and Middle Eastern countries) was approximately 2,000 (Victorian Office of Multicultural Affairs, 2003). Recruitment of the sample was initially through a range of community and social groups, formal ethnic organizations and projects funded by various government and non-government organizations. The sample snowballed from these initial contacts to a total of 255 participants. Given the lack of an existing sampling frame, the recruitment strategy was appropriate for research with refugee communities. A community advisory group (CAG) was constituted with representation from the relevant ethnic community groups, service providers such as women's hospitals and community health and migrant resource centers and government agencies responsible for ethnic health policy formation. The role of the CAG was to assist in the recruitment of the sample; provide a mechanism for feedback and dissemination to and from their communities and agencies; and identify relevant priority issues within the local contexts. The CAG met four times a year but individual members were consulted as required.

The African women in the sample (n = 141) were from Somalia, Ethiopia, Eritrea, Sudan and Nigeria[4] and had been in Australia an average of five years, having emigrated mostly from refugee camps under the women-at-risk program or family reunion programs. The Middle Eastern women (n = 114) also arrived under the humanitarian program mostly for reasons of family reunion and marriage migration and were from Egypt, Lebanon, Iraq, Jordan, Saudi Arabia and Syria with a longer duration of residence–an average of 13 years. In general, the women who participated in the study were between the ages of 19 and 50 years. More than half were married (53%). None of those who were working had been able to find employment that took advantage of their prior qualifications, and their employment was restricted largely to subordinate positions in domestic and other service related industries. This is not atypical for new immigrants to Australia (Markovic & Manderson, 2000). However, it was uniformly perceived as race-related, demonstrated for instance by comments that had been made about their 'obvious' presentation (veils, scarves, *hijab*), "impenetrable accents" and desire to remain different from the host population by continuing to engage with cultural and religious practices. A majority of the women (70%) had 'health care cards' indicative of low income, and a dependency on welfare benefits and state subsidized concessions. Over a third of the women lived in low cost, state subsidized accommodation.

Although they were a widely diverse group in terms of ethnicity, education and other socio-economic indicators, they shared some similarities in cultural backgrounds and family life experience and common experiences of the migration process and in accessing health care services in Australia.

CBPR in data collection. Discussions with women during recruitment found that the women were uncomfortable with the focus on FGC. The national and international profile given to the FGC eradication program had resulted in women from affected communities feeling resentful of being perceived and identified solely as "infibulated women." A practice that traditionally characterized their modesty had been publicized to the extent that they were defined by the structural integrity of their "private parts" (Allotey et al., 2001). While most agreed that reproductive health issues were a major concern, they were more inclined to participate in a research program that was also open to investigating the broader issues that affected their resettlement and broader health and well-being. For instance, in early focus groups to set up the study, many women characterized their experience of and treatment by the health and social services as inherently marginalizing; unless they appeared to be destitute, they could not obtain assistance. They described this as "benevolent racism" and "demeaning." As a result, the level of wariness of the "advocacy industry" was distinct. Similar findings have been reported in other studies of refugee resettlement (Peisker & Tilbury, 2003).

Consequently, while data collection proceeded on the original proposal, the research relationship was negotiated to include a range of other projects initiated by the women. These included a study on parenting difficulties, a joint project with emergency services to identify their needs in relation to domestic and racially motivated violence and safety (Baho & Allotey, 2004) and a review of the work conditions for bicultural workers (Baho, 2005). These became an integral part of a larger research program with the goal of investigating and enabling the health and well-being of resettling refugee women. We describe the development of one of these projects following a summary of the results.

Data analysis. Interviews and focus group discussions were tape recorded and transcribed. Thematic analysis was the main approach to analysis. Data were coded based on themes related to reproductive health. Coding was revised as other themes emerged from ongoing discussions with women in the community. The research team disseminated results to the women predominantly through the CAG, but also through interaction at social gatherings and through annual newsletters targeted at service providers and community groups. The qualitative data were analysed with QSR NUD*IST Software. Coding was done mainly by one of the principal investigators (PA) and discussed in research team meetings.

Results and Discussion

We present a brief summary of the findings as they pertained to FGC to give some context to the concern the women had about research questions that were not a priority for them. Other results of the study are reported elsewhere (Allotey & Manderson, 2003; Allotey et al., 2004; Allotey et al., 2001; Manderson & Allotey, 2003a, 2003b).

Women from the target communities had a high level of understanding and to a large extent, acceptance of the legislation against FGC. They required some clarification about a number of related issues, such as the potential for the clitoris and labia to continue to grow in women who were not excised. The issue of agency was raised in the context of women who had requested re-infibulation following childbirth–a procedure that is illegal under the current FGC legislation. Women perceived this as racist because non-African women are able to undergo procedures such as hymen and labial reconstruction for cosmetic reasons (Allotey et al., 2001). In general, women who had undergone FGC did not perceive themselves as being at higher risk for gynaecological complications. Most of the discussion on complications returned to the definitions of 'normal.' They reported that when reproductive health histories were taken for antenatal care, they were asked questions about painful menstruation and difficulties in passing urine. With their own bodies as their only reference point, most found that these questions either did not make sense or were difficult to answer. Recent mothers of young daughters also described their apprehension about cleaning the genitalia of their infants because of lack of familiarity with unaltered genitals. Indeed, one reported being reprimanded by a maternal health nurse during a six-month postnatal assessment for failing to maintain the hygiene of her daughter adequately.

More significantly for the women, however, was a strong sense of needing to put the discussion of FGC into perspective. For many, perceptions of reproductive health were tempered by previous sexual and reproductive health experiences. Some who had come through refugee camps had to trade sexual favors for food or medicines for themselves and their families as a matter of basic survival. Current priorities in their lives were more important: maintaining constant supplies of basic resources for resettlement of their families, the continued racial and social problems faced by their children as visible minorities, issues of intergenerational family conflict, and concerns about family remaining in conflict areas. The FGC procedure, which had occurred for them when they were very young, was therefore not the most pressing issue. One woman reported "what has happened has happened, it is in the past, why do we have to keep going on about it." While CBPR is founded on the premise of researching what is most important to community members, the Australia data showed that the researchers and the women in the community had different priorities and different long-term goals.

Supporting a mother with an intrauterine death: CBPR in action. This case was chosen because it typifies the range of issues that were of concern to the community and illustrates the importance of advocacy and research approaches that enable prompt intervention.

Mrs. A (gravida 1, para 0) from Eritrea reported to the antenatal clinic of a women's hospital for a routine antenatal check at approximately the 25th week of her pregnancy. She had missed her last appointment by a week because of a death in her community. The bicultural worker, who also acted as an interpreter, accompanied her into the obstetrician's consulting room. During her examination, the obstetrician was unable to hear a fetal heart beat, and Mrs. A could not remember precisely when she had last felt any fetal movements. She was sent to have an ultrasound, a procedure that she had consistently refused prior to that because of her concern that it might harm the fetus. Through translation of the obstetrician's advice, the bicultural worker explained the importance of the ultrasound to determine fetal problems. Mrs. A finally consented and an intrauterine death was confirmed. However, Mrs. A was then told that no beds were available and she would need to return the next day for a termination of her pregnancy.

Distressed, Mrs. A could not understand why, despite her position in the hospital, the bicultural worker did not react against a client being sent home with a "dead baby inside her." She returned the next day for an induction of labor. She was again accompanied by the bicultural worker who explained that she had to be de-infibulated[5] prior to the delivery as was the normal procedure for infibulated women (RACOG, 1997). The bicultural worker was then called away to another client. Following the birth, Mrs. A was presented with the dead fetus and left alone with it; again this was then normal hospital procedure to enable a healthy grieving process (Hughes & Riches, 2003; Hughes, Turton, Hopper, & Evans, 2002; Leon, 1992). Only after about 10 minutes of distressed calls was she finally able to communicate to the staff that she wanted the dead fetus to be removed from the room. When the bicultural worker returned to visit, Mrs. A expressed her disappointment that the bicultural worker had not explained the inappropriateness of leaving her with a corpse to the hospital staff. In reporting the events, Mrs. A described the whole experience as one of the worst in her life, surpassing anything she had experienced as a displaced person.

For Mrs. A, the experience highlighted her powerlessness within a system that she did not understand. She had been given no support to deal with the still birth and had not understood the purpose of being "abandoned with a dead fetus." Most importantly for her, however, was the sense that the one person she could have relied on, the bicultural worker, was not available and had let this happen to her.

This and other supporting cases resulted in the researchers taking a strong advocacy role and working with the women to make presentations to various agencies regarding their needs and to initiate a number of further research projects (Allotey & Manderson, 2003). One of these was an exploration of the position of bicultural workers. Under the Australian policy of multiculturalism, agencies were encouraged and often funded to employ staff from ethnic minority backgrounds to deal with the issues that affect clients from those ethnic backgrounds (Commonwealth of Australia, 1998). Within the implementation of the Family and Reproductive Rights Education Program (FARREP, the Victorian State strategy for the National FGM program), the FARREP workers were critical to ensuring that the needs of infibulated women were met within clinical and other health related settings. The FARREP workers were attached to hospitals and community health centers around Melbourne that had significant clientele from the target communities. In hospitals, FARREP workers were expected to support women in all areas of their clinical encounter, both as interpreters and cultural brokers.

However, focus group discussions with bicultural workers revealed that their roles within the work place were unclear and lacked organizational support with no prospects for career advancement. Their skills levels were variable ranging from medical practitioners unable to get their qualifications recognized to those with no formal qualifications. The main essential "skills" in the job description were their ethnicity (loosely defined as country of birth) and language proficiencies. As a result of the lack of preparation for their role, they often found themselves in situations in which they felt uncomfortable proposing interventions to clients that could create "cultural discomfort." They found that women from their communities would accept their translation of physician explanations as an implicit recommendation from the bicultural worker. In spite of an expectation that bicultural workers would be advocates for their communities, the workers usually felt unable to question the authority of their employers in order to represent the needs of the clients. Similar observations have been made in research in the United States and the United Kingdom in the development of community health worker models of primary care delivery (Corkery et al., 1997; Musser-Granski & Carrillo, 1997; Tribe, 1999). However, in spite of ongoing funding for bicultural workers in Australia, the efficacy of their roles remains poorly investigated and evaluated as an intervention. The research presented here was critical in facilitating a review of bicultural workers in general (ongoing) and of the conditions for FARREP workers in particular (Baho, 2005). In addition, a group of FARREP workers, supported by the research team and women from their communities, have initiated a series of workshops for assertiveness and leadership training.

STUDY 2: NEW ZEALAND

Similar to Australia, in the early 1990s refugee women from countries where FGC is practiced began arriving in New Zealand, drawing attention to this previously unheard-of practice. Within only a few years, FGC was criminalized with an amendment to the Crimes Act (1996). It was not until 1998 that a one time only education program was implemented in New Zealand for health professionals. Education programs for affected communities (unevaluated) have appeared sporadically but have generally been based in one city in New Zealand, while the women live in four main cities and do not have access to these programs. Compared with Australia, New Zealand has minimal, if any, cultural support for refugee women in the health care system and this varies widely between cities in New Zealand.

Methods

The New Zealand study[6] was initiated by a group of well-regarded, elder women leaders from the Somali community who approached the research team (which includes both Somali and non-Somali members) and requested research that would represent their views on FGC. They wanted the voices of the women to be documented in safe and appropriate ways. The project received ethical approval from the University of Waikato Psychology Department Ethics Committee. Informed consent was obtained from all participants in accordance with the approved protocol.

Sample. Data were collected in two phases. In this paper, we will focus on the findings from Phase 2 as they more directly related to the theme of advocacy. Details of Phase 1 and results can be found elsewhere (Guerin & Elmi, 2004, 2005). Briefly, the first phase of the project was larger and more comprehensive, with both quantitative and qualitative data collected using semi-structured interviews between December 2003 and January 2004. A total of 54 women from a wide range of age groups (16-50 + years) from four different cities in New Zealand were recruited initially through community networks and then through snowball sampling. A convenience sample of ten women participated in either small focus groups or were individually interviewed during Phase 2. These were conducted between September 2004 and January 2005. These women were not necessarily participants in Phase 1 and they ranged in age from 27 to 48 years and were from two cities in New Zealand. This phase focused on presenting women with the results of the Phase 1 and gaining their feedback about the project and their impressions of the accuracy of the data from Phase 1. All participants were provided with $10.00 grocery vouchers after the interviews or focus groups. A number of years of research and consultation with the women in this community found that some form of compensation or gift for participation in research was appropriate and expected.

Data collection. Interviews and focus groups were conducted almost exclusively in the homes of the participant. Interviews were conducted independently by one of two female, multi-lingual interviewers in the language preferred by the participant (usually Somali or English). Because FGC is illegal in New Zealand, no interviews were audio-taped, and no questions were asked that could potentially reveal illegal activity. Data collected during Phase 1 included demographic information about the participant, ancestry, knowledge about the practice of FGC, knowledge and views about media and publicity relating to FGC, views about medicalization of FGC, personal experience, ideas or experience in relation to continuing FGC with their daughters, views and knowledge about educational programs and the laws. While interviewers generally followed a semi-structured interview guide, they were encouraged to allow participants to have relaxed conversations about the general topic of FGC.

Data analysis. Interviewers took diligent notes, with word-for-word quotes when possible. These were later typed into an Excel spreadsheet and were analyzed for general themes and frequency of occurrence where appropriate. The two main researchers (PG & FE) hand coded and discussed the results and interpretation at length from these Excel spreadsheets. When necessary, interviewers re-contacted participants if any comments were unclear. We present a brief summary of results from Phase 1 with a focus on the comments from Phase 2.

Results and Discussion

In contrast to Australia, the topic of FGC in New Zealand was generally either biased against the practice or 'silent' (i.e., not discussed at all), but an issue that Somali women wanted prioritized, as they felt that they were not involved in important decisions that affected them and their Somali identity. Overall, we found that the prevalence of Type I circumcision, or *Sunna* was higher in the younger population with one third reporting having had Type I in the 16-35 year age group but none with Type I in the older age groups. All the others reported Type III circumcisions. The majority of women reported positive experiences with only two women reporting negative experiences. The two women who reported negative effects reported having Type III and none of the women who had Type I reported any negative effects. For the two women who reported negative effects of their circumcision, one was supportive of Type I circumcision and the other replied, "I don't know. Not for me, but maybe for others."

Most women had never attended a FGC-related education program in New Zealand or overseas. About half thought the programs were necessary and most suggested that education programs should target health professionals about FGC and the Somali culture. The majority of women reported knowing about the laws, but that they had never been formally provided with this information, and most felt that these laws were unfair and harsh. Nearly all of the women wanted FGC to be legalized in New Zealand, but only Type I.

Participants in Phase 2 agreed with the results of Phase 1. Of interest for this paper, were a few of the general discussion comments and the implications of these for advocacy and future programs in New Zealand. For example, one woman said:

> *Women should have the right to practice their culture without running away from New Zealand and they should have someone they trust to discuss and talk to about cutting and what possibilities are there for their issue to be discussed in legal terms, without fear of being watched or spied on if ever you go out of the country?*

Another woman felt very differently, saying,

> *Women should be told and educated on how circumcision has not done any of the things that they think it was performed for in the*

first place and that if they don't do it to their girls, they will not be affected at all. I think it's the women who worry more than the young girls.

The comments documented in Phase 2 revealed the subtleties of discrimination and the feelings of marginalization in their new country. For example, this woman said:

. . . Western countries take children and women [refugees] more because they can brainwash them with their wrong ideas on circumcision. They will do anything to make Somalis follow Western practices but at the same time, because they cannot change how you look, they will still call you names like 'black' and 'go home you fucking black.' When people say you can't practice your culture anymore, simply, they are telling you to go away indirectly: they don't want your culture and they don't want you.

Another woman's comments reflected the distrust of authorities and the complicated nature of working through the issues of identity.

I had Sunna and if I have daughters and if they are not cut it will not be a problem unless it starts affecting their identity or they become outcasts. See, my mother had Type III; I had Sunna. I will want Sunna for my daughters if it's acceptable here, but if not, then I will not bother like those women who are saving up to take their daughters out of the country in the future. They don't know they are being spied on and whatever they do and wherever they go they will be caught because the kids will tell the teacher about their holiday and what happened. New Zealand teachers are government spies and they ask the children all the information.

Participants in Phase 2 indicated concern about the mothers of daughters who were not yet circumcised and how they were going to negotiate solutions to what they saw as a very serious problem in a hostile climate.

We should be able to cut our girls without fear of being jailed. We should be able to talk freely about our feelings without fear. Now we worry if you discuss this, your name will be recorded and even if you go out of New Zealand we fear that our daughters will be investigated whether they had been circumcised.

GENERAL DISCUSSION

In broad terms, the content of these studies address similar issues about the reproductive health of refugee women from countries where FGC is practiced. The voyeurism and arguably, the cultural imperialism raised by interest in FGC (Bridgeman & Millns, 1995; Kluge, 1996; Obermeyer, 1999; Parker, 1995; Sheldon & Wilkinson, 1998) remains a cause for the reaction of communities against programs that address the health and underlying gender inequalities assumed to be associated with FGC. However, the context of distrust experienced by many refugee women and disempowerment faced by ethnic minority groups within a dominant health and welfare sector, underscore the need for approaches that value genuine community participation.

Participatory action research combines participatory research, the goal of which is community led structural transformation, with action research, which involves an iterative process of acting on, evaluating research findings and revising research aims, thus creating a dynamic research process. The approach lends itself to working across cultural groups and particularly with disadvantaged communities to ensure that the research is ethical and non-exploitative (Khanlou & Peter, 2005; Minkler, 2004). As was evident in both studies presented here, the involvement of communities is critical in defining the research.

In the New Zealand study, CBPR enabled women in the resettling communities with the support of researcher advocates to initiate the building of an evidence base documenting their views on FGC. The New Zealand researchers have presented the work to government, agencies, community groups, as well as academics, both nationally and internationally, but are finding that influencing the quickly implemented legislation and policy, and corresponding misconceptions, is a more difficult task.

The FARREP program in Australia was developed on the basis of community consultation (Baho, 2005), but the implementation through FARREP workers found that the bicultural worker model did not take account of the ability of the workers to advocate on behalf of the clients on culturally sensitive and emotive issues. Again the CBPR approach has been critical in enabling these subtle but important issues to be identified.

Research limitations. The issue of representative sampling in hard to reach communities continues to remain a challenge in the generalizability of research findings. This is important to consider in CBPR because even at the community level, the voices represented through advocacy are the ones that are able to obtain access to researchers and the research process. The importance of relationship building in this type of research, the use of known community members as researchers (Guerin, Abdi, & Guerin, 2003; Guerin & Elmi, 2004) and the multiple roles played by researchers also have implications for the "objectivity" of data generated (Allotey & Manderson, 2003) and these issues need to be further explored in CBPR as this area of research gains increased currency. Another limitation is the potential that women will provide socially acceptable responses. Guerin and Elmi (2004) describe the complex multiple influences that bear on the telling of personal stories or interview responses, including cultural, social and legal histories and present contexts. They also discuss how responses can be interpreted or mis-interpreted from the same influences on interviewers and research-ers.

Advocacy. The researcher-as-advocate potentially plays a dual role in the CBPR method–as advocates at an individual level within communities and as contributors to addressing policy concerns (Johnston & Allotey, 2003). Advocacy on the personal level during research projects serves a number of functions, both for the researcher and for those receiving the advocacy. For the researcher, participating with women in the community as an advocate is a good way to understand the subtleties of discrimination, the pressures and hassles of day-to-day life for many refugee women, and is a way of developing trust with the women in the community. For the refugee woman, having the researcher-as-advocate helps on a practical level, but also, less obviously, it can provide a learning opportunity of how to do things in a 'Western way.'

Advocacy at a policy level is a final way of 'completing the process,' in that the issues revealed through personal advocacy and research results can potentially be corrected. It is this step in the process that is often missed out by researchers, although it may not always be necessary. However, for marginalized and vulnerable women, this is a critical step in closing the loop. Tiilikainen (2002) explores this issue in her work with Somali women in Finland stressing the need for research to have a purpose and usefulness, especially for groups such as these.

Implementing CBPR research with refugee women also requires considerations in terms of ethics, funding and dissemination that often extends beyond what is required in Western-based research. Both studies described here showed how the researcher-as-advocate became an essential role when working with people who have unmet needs and issues that the researcher can, minimally, facilitate. But this researcher-as-advocate role also requires a re-thinking of the professional boundaries often surrounding research, such as being a neutral observer documenting information. The obligation of the researcher to assist where there is a need is often a reality in research with groups such as these (Lammers, 2005). Finally, dissemination of research results can require a greater amount of creativity, time and cost for the researcher. Some refugee women who do not read or write, even in their own language, require oral dissemination of results and those who do not read English require translated reports. For the research to have an empowering aim for the communities involved, they will need to have the results provided in appropriate ways, but may also need assistance with the next steps in ensuring that the research has positive outcomes, such as contributing to the development of programs, interventions, and policy.

NOTES

1. Female genital cutting is used here to refer to the range of cultural practices that involve varying degrees of excision and infibulation of parts of the female genitalia. 'Cutting' is used in preference to the previously used 'mutilation' to avoid an implicit value judgement. This had been a significant issue with women who participated in our study (see for instance Allotey, Manderson, & Grover, 2001). The WHO classifies four types, (Type I, II, III, and IV), but only Type I and Type III were relevant in this study. Type I is generally the most "mild" ("excision of the prepuce with or without excision of part or all of the clitoris") and is sometimes called *Sunna*, which means "tradition," in some practicing communities. Type III is perhaps the most "severe" with "excision of part or all of the external genitalia and stitching/narrowing of the vaginal opening" and is also called *infibulation* or *Pharaonic* circumcision (Guerin & Elmi, 2004).

2. 'Refugee women' is used for brevity. 'Women from refugee backgrounds' would more accurately describe the participants with whom we worked.

3. This study was funded by a 3-year grant from the National Health and Medical Research Council of Australia (NH&MRC 990360). Principal investigators were Lenore Manderson and Pascale Allotey.

4. Nigeria is obviously not in the Horn, but the women in sample were closely associated with the target community and had also undergone FGC.

5. Women who have been infibulated are often de-infibulated prior to marriage (to facilitate first intercourse) or prior to childbirth. Some women prefer to be re-sutured or re-infibulated following childbirth (Allotey, Manderson & Grover, 2001).

6. This work was supported by a grant from the New Zealand Foundation for Research, Science and Technology (UOWX0203, Strangers in Town: Enhancing Family and Community in a More Diverse New Zealand Society) and a small grant from the Faculty of Arts and Social Sciences, University of Waikato.

REFERENCES

Allotey, P., & Manderson, L. (2003). Case studies to case work: Ethical obligations in research with refugee women. In P. Allotey (Ed.), The health of refugees: Public health perspectives from crisis to settlement (pp. 200-211). Melbourne: Oxford University Press.

Allotey, P., Manderson, L., Baho, S., & Demian, L. (2004). Reproductive health for re-settling refugee and migrant women. Journal of Health Issues, 78(Autumn 2004), 12-17.

Allotey, P., Manderson, L., & Grover, S. (2001). The politics of female genital surgery in displaced communities. Critical Public Health, 11(3), 189-201.

Baho, S. (2005). Providing reproductive rights health promotion to resettling refugee women: An evaluation of the Family and Reproductive Rights Education Program. Unpublished Masters of Women's Health, The University of Melbourne, Melbourne.

Baho, S., & Allotey P. (2004). Staying Safe. Horn of African women's experience of the emergency services in Victoria. Melbourne. Department of Justice Victoria

Barnett, L. (2002). Global Governance and the Evolution of the International Refugee Regime. International Journal of Refugee Law, 14, 238-257.

Beiser, M., & Feng, H. (2001). Language acquisition, unemployment and depressive disorder among Southeast Asian refugees. Social Science and Medicine, 53, 1321-1334.

Bridgeman, J. E., & Millns, S. E. (1995). Law and body politics: Regulating the female body. London: Dartmouth.

Callamard, A. (1999). Refugee women: A gendered and political analysis of the refugee experience. In A. Ager (Ed.), Refugees: Perspectives on the experience of forced migration (pp. 196-214). London: Continuum.

Commonwealth of Australia. (1998). Charter of Public Service in a Culturally Diverse Society. Canberra: Australian Government Publishing Service.

Corkery, E., Palmer, C., Foley, M. E., Schechter, C. B., Frisher, L., & Roman, S. H. (1997). Effect of bicultural community health worker on completion of diabetes education in a hispanic population. Diabetes Care, 20(3), 254-257.

Daniel, E. V., & Knusden, J. C. (1995). Mistrusting refugees. Berkley: University of California Press.

Guerin, B., Abdi, A., & Guerin, P. B. (2003). Health status of Somali refugees living in Hamilton and their experiences with the medical system. NZ J of Psychology, 32, 27-32.

Guerin, P. B., Diiriye, R. O., Corrigan, C., & Guerin, B. (2003). Physical activity programs for refugee Somali women: Working out in a new country. Women & Health, 38, 83-99.

Guerin, P. B., & Elmi, F. H. (2005). Somali women's views of female circumcision. On the Frontiers: New public goods research on population, migration and community dynamics conference in March/April, Wellington. Available from www.waikato. ac.nz/wfass/migration.

Guerin, P. B., & Elmi, F. H. (2004). The analysis of female circumcision stories: The uses and abuses of oral histories. Oral History in New Zealand, 16, 9-16.

Guerin, B., Guerin, P. B., Diiriye, R. O., & Abdi, A. (2004). Living in a close community: The everyday life of Somali refugees. Network, 16, 7-17.

Hughes, P., & Riches, S. (2003). Psychological aspects of perinatal loss. Current Opinion in Obstetrics & Gynecology, 15(2), 107-111.

Hughes, P., Turton, P., Hopper, E., & Evans, C. D. H. (2002). Assessment of guidelines for good practice in psychosocial care of mothers after stillbirth. Lancet, 360(9327), 114-118.

Johnston, V., & Allotey, P. (2003). Mobilizing the 'chattering classes' for advocacy in Australia. Development, 46, 75-80.

Khanlou, N., & Peter, E. (2005). Participatory action research: Considerations for ethical review. Social Science and Medicine, 60, 2333-2340.

Kluge, E. W. (1996). Female genital mutilation, cultural values and ethics. Journal of Obstetrics and Gynaecology Abingdon, 16(2), 71-76.

Knight, R., Hotchin, A., Bayly, C., & Grover, S. (1999). Female genital mutilation–experience of The Royal Women's Hospital, Melbourne. Aust N Z J Obstet Gynaecol, 39, 50-54.

Lammers, E. (2005). Refugees, asylum seekers and anthropologists: The taboo on giving. Global Migration Perspectives (no. 29). Global Commission on International Migration. Accessed from www.gcim.org on 15 June 2005.

Leon, I. G. (1992). Perinatal loss–a critique of current hospital practices. Clinical Pediatrics, 31(6), 366-374.

Manderson, L., & Allotey, P. (2003a). The cultural politics of competence in Australian health services. Anthropology in Medicine, 10(1), 70-85.

Manderson, L., & Allotey, P. (2003b). Story telling, marginality and community in Australia: How immigrants position their differences in health care settings. Medical Anthropology, 22(1), 1-21.

Manderson, L., Kelaher, M., Markovic, M., & McManus, K. (1998). A woman without a man is a woman at risk: Women at risk in Australian Humanitarian Programs. Journal of Refugee Studies, 11(3), 267-283.

Markovic, M., & Manderson, L. (2000). European immigrants and the Australian labor market. A case study on women from the Former Yugoslavia. Journal of Ethnic and Migration Studies, 26, 127-136.

Minkler, M. (2004). Ethical challenges for the "outside" researcher in community-based participatory research. Health Educ Behav, 31(6), 684-697.

Musser-Granski, J., & Carrillo, D. F. (1997). The use of bilingual, bicultural paraprofessionals in mental health services: Issues for hiring, training and supervision. Community Mental Health Journal, 33(1), 51-60.

NZIS. (2004). Refugee Voices. Wellington: New Zealand Immigration Service.

Obermeyer, C. (1999). Female genital surgeries: The known, the unknown and the unknowable. Medical Anthropology Quarterly, 13(1), 79-106.

Parker, M. (1995). Rethinking female circumcision. Africa, 64(4), 506-523.

Peisker, V. C., & Tilbury, F. (2003). "Active" and "passive" resettlement: Support services and refugees' own resources on resettlement style. International Migration, 41, 61-91.

RACOG. (1997). Female Genital Mutilation. Information for Australian health professionals. East Melbourne: Royal Australian College of Obstetricians and Gynaecologists.

Sheldon, S., & Wilkinson, S. (1998). Female genital mutilation and cosmetic surgery: Regulating non-therapeutic body modification. Bioethics, 12(4), 263-285.

Tiilikainen, M. (2002). Homes and fields, friends and informants: Fieldwork among Somali refugee women. In H. Pesonen, T. Sakaranaho, T. Sjoblom & T. Utriainen, (eds.). Styles and Positions: Ethnographic perspectives in comparative religion. Helsinki: University of Helsinki.

Tribe, R. (1999). Bridging the gap or damming the flow? Some observations on using interpreters/bicultural workers when working with refugee clients, many of whom have been tortured. British Journal of Medical Psychology, 72, 567-576.

UNHCR. (2005). 2004 Global Refugee Trends. Geneva: United Nations High Commissioner for Refugees.

Verdirame, G., Harrell-Bond, B., Lomo, Z., & Garry, H. (2005). Rights in exile. Janus Faced Humanitarianism (Vol. 17). Oxford: Berghahn Books.

Victorian Office of Multicultural Affairs. (2003). Community Profiles 2001 Census Volumes 1-4. Melbourne: Victorian Office of Multicultural Affairs, Department of Victorian Communities.

doi:10.1300/J013v43n04_02

Typologies of Rural Lay-Health Advocacy Among Rural Women in Australia

Narelle Warren, BA(Hons), BSc
Milica Markovic, PhD
Lenore Manderson, PhD

SUMMARY. *Background:* Public health advocacy effects changes in health behaviors and outcomes through applying health promotion expertise to specific groups. Advocacy occurs through the provision of tools to empower those who are either experiencing, or at risk of, a particular health status.

Research objectives: Health care experiences of women living in rural Victoria, Australia, were explored in the context of generally poor access to reproductive health services. Women's experiences are investigated within the theoretical framework of lay-health advocacy, i.e., relying on individual health care experience and knowledge to promote and improve the health care of others.

Methodology: The study applied a qualitative design, and a self-identified sample of women was recruited through network sampling techniques. Fifty-seven women participated in in-depth interviews.

Narelle Warren, Milica Markovic, and Lenore Manderson are affiliated with the School of Psychology, Psychiatry and Psychological Medicine, Faculty of Medicine, Nursing and Health Sciences, Monash University.

Address correspondence to: Lenore Manderson, PhD, FASSA, School of Psychology, Psychiatry and Psychological Medicine, Monash University (Caulfield Campus), 900 Dandenong Road, Caulfield East, Victoria 3145, Australia (E-mail: lenore.manderson@med.monash.edu.au).

[Haworth co-indexing entry note]: "Typologies of Rural Lay-Health Advocacy Among Rural Women in Australia." Warren, Narelle, Milica Markovic, and Lenore Manderson. Co-published simultaneously in *Women & Health* (The Haworth Medical Press, an imprint of The Haworth Press, Inc.) Vol. 43, No. 4, 2006, pp. 27-47; and: *Women's Health: New Frontiers in Advocacy & Social Justice Research* (ed: Elizabeth Cartwright, and Pascale Allotey) The Haworth Medical Press, an imprint of The Haworth Press, Inc., 2006, pp. 27-47. Single or multiple copies of this article are available for a fee from The Haworth Document Delivery Service [1-800-HAWORTH, 9:00 a.m. - 5:00 p.m. (EST). E-mail address: docdelivery@haworthpress.com].

Results: Three types of lay-health advocacy emerged. *Advocacy-seekers* expected the researchers to use their experiences of poor health care to educate health professionals to provide better quality care. *Advocacy-providers* used their knowledge and experiences to take an active part in promoting the health care of other women. *Story-tellers* expected their narratives to empower other women or unidentified social groups to feel less isolated in their health care experiences.

Discussion: In providing narratives of their health care, women were critical of social inequalities facing people living in rural Australia. Lay-health advocates offer a cost-effective and appropriate option for reducing adverse health outcomes within resource-poor settings. Informed by women's narratives, we suggest strategies to enhance rural women's health care. doi:10.1300/J013v43n04_03 *[Article copies available for a fee from The Haworth Document Delivery Service: 1-800-HAWORTH. E-mail address: <docdelivery@haworthpress.com> Website: <http://www. HaworthPress.com>* © *2006 by The Haworth Press, Inc. All rights reserved.]*

KEYWORDS. Australia, gynecological health, reproductive health, rural women, typology of advocacy

BACKGROUND

Historically, public health advocacy effected changes in the health status of individuals and communities through enhancing access to services, information, and treatments (Hawe & Shiell, 2000; Mechanic, 1999). Accordingly, professionals have introduced changes to improve population health outcomes (Bybee & Sullivan, 2002; McFarlane & Wiist, 1997; Sullivan & Bybee, 1999). Recent health promotion initiatives emphasize involving other community members in identifying appropriate health interventions and responding to these. In this context, Carlisle's (2000) conceptual framework distinguishes four distinct types of advocacy: 'Representation,' operating on the level of individual or group cases and drawing upon medical evidence, seeks to prevent specific health conditions. 'Social policy reform' efforts are directed at structural factors, and address the cause(s) of ill-health at the policy (or governmental) level. 'Community development' occurs when the health promotion practitioner works with an individual or a group to address health concerns through enabling individuals or groups to make positive health-related decisions. 'Community activism' employs similar objectives and directs these at the structural level; such advocacy seeks to provide communities with skills to affect health-related policies. In Australia, the national breast cancer and cervical screening programs (introduced in 1991 and 1995, respectively) exemplify 'representation' and 'social policy reform' initiatives. The FARREP (Family and Reproductive Rights Education Program), a national education program on female genital mutilation, is an example of 'community development.' The National Ovarian Cancer Network (OvCa Australia), which aims to raise the awareness of ovarian cancer, falls under 'community activism.'

Lay-health advocacy, the focus of this paper, is not part of Carlisle's framework, but we build on it and incorporate some aspects of Carlisle's advocacy, for example 'community action.' Lay-health advocacy occurs when the woman is an advocate for her own health or for the benefit of others (see, for example, Burling & Webb, 2005). Sharing health-related experiences facilitates an understanding of the condition for the experiencing person and members of her social networks, increases awareness of others' coping strategies, treatment-related advice, and implications of the condition, and (perhaps most importantly) allows the experiencing person to know she is not alone in her experience. Lay-health advocacy not only refers to people's ability to represent themselves, but to how they access services and secure the support of others who can act as advocates on their behalf. Participation in disease-specific patient support groups (including peer advocates, see Mead, Hilton, & Curtis, 2001) or contact with paid community health advocates (such as FARREP workers) may influence lay-health advocacy. Health advocacy is informal and often provided by members of women's own social support networks, ensuring that patients receive relevant information and psycho-social support. In some situations, people who have experienced a particular health condition become powerful advocates for others with a similar condition. Wilson, Anderson and Meischke (2000) found that women who had survived breast cancer were not only able to advocate for their own health following treatment and recovery, but many also became advocates for others with breast cancer. In this paper, we refer to such women as lay-health advocates.

Self-advocacy and peer-advocacy are two types of lay-health advocacy. Self-advocacy is usually concerned with a particular health issue (e.g., disability: Block, Skeels, Keys, & Rimmer, 2005; Palmer, 2000)– it brings together people with that condition and seeks to prevent their discrimination; the members organize themselves. Similarly, peer-advocacy is established around a particular health problem (e.g., HIV/ AIDS (Paxton, 2002); substance abuse) but is driven by (community) health services (see Mead et al., 2001). Peers receive formal training then train others. Lay-health advocacy has a broader scope, focusing on improving the overall health experience of people, regardless of their particular health problem; personal experience rather than training drives it.

Lay-health advocacy is particularly important for rural populations. Compared with urban women, mid-life women in rural and remote parts of Australia had poorer access to health services, and are more likely to feel that their interactions with health professionals were inadequate (Brown, Young, & Byles, 1999). People in rural areas of Australia, where this research was conducted, have lower life expectancy, higher fertility and higher rates of hospitalization than those in urban areas (AIHW, 1998; Government of Victoria, 2004). In contrast to urban areas, the bulk of health services and information provision is delivered by nursing professionals rather than medical practitioners (AIHW, 1998); this impacts upon access to formal health advocacy.

Research objectives. Reflecting our interest in the link between advocacy and health outcomes, in this paper we explore the health care experiences of Australian rural women and investigate the role of lay-health advocacy.

METHODOLOGY

The data on which we draw were obtained from a study on the search for diagnosis and adaptation to living with a range of woman-specific health problems, such as endometriosis, hysterectomy, oophorectomy, poly-cystic ovarian syndrome, premature ovarian failure, unresolved infertility, common serious disorders of pregnancy (e.g., pre-eclampsia, fetal growth restriction, placenta previa, miscarriages, and pre-term labour and delivery), and breast-feeding difficulties.[1] These health conditions all affect women's mental as well as physical health, since they challenge women's own conceptions of their wellbeing, biological capacity and, often, expectations for the future (Boughton, 2002; Kitzinger & Willmott, 2002)–hence the title of the project, 'Disrupting the idea of woman,' which we used in media and information provided to potential participants. The project was approved by a university ethics committee.

Women of all ages were recruited throughout Victoria, Australia. Between September 2003 and June 2004, a media release describing the project and researchers was sent to the editors of 42 community newspapers. Information about the project appeared as an advertisement or a news article. Media releases were also reproduced in the quarterly newsletters of four regional and two urban women's health services; the Victorian government-run Rural Women's Network also included information about the project in its monthly e-bulletin. In some instances, women heard about the study through their social networks.

The research project was partly envisaged as advocating for women by providing them with opportunities to tell their story about women's health problems, as indicated above, that were stigmatizing to some extent and for which little formal social support was available, particularly for rural women. We ensured advocacy information dissemination by providing the names and contact details of appropriate and empathetic health professionals outside women's immediate residential area. Alternatively, we provided women with health promotional materials from the Women's Health Information Centre, a state-wide health information service, or the 'Better Health Channel,' a health information service endorsed by the Victorian government.

Participation was voluntary, and women did not receive payment or gifts for their involvement in the study. Women who had experienced one of the health conditions described were included; all women who enquired about the study met these criteria and all provided informed consent to participate. The total sample included 80 women, 57 of whom lived outside metropolitan Melbourne (the state capital). The 33 remaining women resided within urban areas; given this paper's focus on rural women, these participants were excluded from the analyses presented here.

In interviews, participants were invited to tell their story, from which the authors developed further questions. Basic socio-demographic information was also collected. Interviews were tape-recorded and transcribed verbatim, and transcripts returned to participants unamended for their validation or amendment. Transcripts were coded thematically using Atlas-ti version 5.0 (2004)–to identify commonalities in women's narratives, leading to grounded theory development, i.e., emic perspective (Glaser & Strauss, 1967). Data were de-identified, and pseudonyms were used throughout this paper to maintain anonymity. Socio-demographic data were analyzed using SPSS version 11.0 (2001).

RESULTS

Socio-demographic characteristics of the study participants are displayed in Table 1. The average age of participants was 44.9 years (median 43 years, range 20-88 years). Highly educated women were over-represented: over half (n = 31) had at least a college degree, which suggested that women's willingness to volunteer in research partly related to their educational level and familiarity with the research endeavor. Representativeness of the sample was limited due to low levels of participants from a non-English speaking background (3 women only) and large numbers of married women (n = 39).

TABLE 1. Socio-demographic characteristics of study sample

Age	N	Current occupation+	N
20-29 years	5	Managers/administrators	4
30-39	12	Professionals	20
40-49	24	Associate professionals	4
50-59	11	Intermediate clerical, sales, service	8
60-69	1	Elementary clerical, sales, service	1
70-79	3	Laborers and related workers	2
80-89	1	Other (incl. student, home duties, retired)	18
Country of birth		**Marital status**	
Australia/Oceania	52	Married	39
Western Europe	3	De facto	5
North America	1	Divorced/separated	7
South Africa	1	Single/never married	6
Highest level of education		**Condition***	
Primary	1	Endometriosis	22
Some secondary	10	Hysterectomy/Oophorectomy	36
Completed secondary	5	Pregnancy disorders/loss	21
Technical/business college/training	10	Infertility	9
Tertiary	16	PCOS	5
Post-graduate	15	Early menopause	3
		Other	6

+(Source: ABS, 1997)
*Many participants reported more than one condition, hence numbers add up to greater than study population.

Occupation was classified using the Australian Standard Classification of Occupations, developed by the Australian Bureau of Statistics (ABS, 1997). Many women had no classifiable occupation, due to retirement (n = 9) or full-time participation in 'domestic duties' (n = 8). Over one-third (n = 24) were professionals or managers. Similarly, many (n = 24) worked in a health-related occupation; 15 were nurses; others included community health workers, psychologists and personal care personnel. Many women had had several of the conditions in which we were interested; this accounted for discrepancies between the total participants for each condition and the sample size.

Given the emphasis on advocacy during recruitment, it was unsurprising that women typically identified their reasons for participation in relation to advocacy–they either acted as informal advocates for others or received support provided by the researchers. Others participated because they wanted to be an 'intermediary,' whereby their involvement in the study generated support for other women while they received similar support from the researchers. The latter two groups of women saw the researchers as intermediary between themselves and service providers. Almost without exception, participants expected their involvement to influence other women's experiences with gynecological and reproductive health care. These trends emerged during qualitative data analysis and three broad typologies of self-health advocates were developed: 'advocacy-seekers,' 'advocacy-providers,' and 'story-tellers.' Participants' narratives were placed in typologies depending on (where relevant) the reasons they identified for participation and the themes and issues raised during interviews.

'Advocacy-Seekers'

In the absence of formal health advocacy, many women saw participation as a means of learning from other women's stories. For example, Sophie, who had received very little social or instrumental support during treatment for endometriosis, said, "I'm really interested to find out where you go with this research . . . what other people have to say about their experiences." Many advocacy-seekers had unresolved issues arising from their encounters with health professionals. Some women had experienced difficulties related to diagnosis near their participation in our study, as was the case for Felicity.

Felicity, a mother of three young children, had been informed that she had undergone early menopause (at 36 years) just prior to our interview, yet had not received any information on the implications of her diagnosis–low libido, drier hair and skin, and weight gain–or on-going health management–e.g., her screening behaviors. None of her health care professionals had provided her with such advice, due to their lack of expertise with early menopause, despite that she had traveled to specialist health centers. Around that time, she had found a lump in her breast and informed her general practitioner (GP) about it. He had told her that she was too young for a government-subsidized mammogram–she should go home and not worry; this exacerbated her distress. Felicity hoped that by participating in the study, she could obtain relevant health information. Following her interview, we sent her detailed information explaining the health implications of early menopause, and referred her to an early menopause peer support group and a health information day in a public hospital in Melbourne. At this program, several health and allied-health professionals, as well as a complementary health practitioner (naturopath/herbalist), discussed and answered women's questions about early menopause. This provided Felicity with skills to become a lay-health advocate–she learned how to look after her own health. Finally, after consultation with a breast health specialist, we informed her who to contact for further investigation of the lump in her breast.

Other advocacy-seeking women had either finished or were undergoing treatment for their condition at the time of their participation in their study. Involvement in this study provided them with a way to seek answers to various unresolved questions. For Simone, a 20-year old woman with endometriosis, questions around future fertility remained unanswered and caused distress, which led to her participation in our study.

Simone was diagnosed with endometriosis at 17 years of age and, subsequently, underwent four laparoscopies to remove adhesions. Although her doctor had discussed future fertility with her, she felt his explanations were unsatisfactory. He advised her that, as endometriosis often affects fertility, she should maximize her chances of getting pregnant and have children "sooner rather than later," but also commented that she was currently 'too young' to worry about fertility. She was consequently confused about what "sooner" meant, and whether or not to start attempting conception immediately. Her confusion was heightened by what she had learned on the Internet and from friends' experiences:

> [The doctors] say [you're] too young; you don't have to worry about it yet . . . I guess just from talking to other people, if they've

had the same thing you believe them a bit more. One of my friend's sisters had it, and she had her kids straight away. She said [the decision] was really hard, and you think you could just listen to the doctor and not worry about it and then, say you waited 10 years and you couldn't have kids, you'd blame yourself . . . I'd rather know the risks with fertility and stuff, if you should have kids, if you should, what you should be doing . . . I really wanted someone to say, yes have kids or don't, but I know they can't do it.

Simone hoped the researchers would be able to answer this question. Although we could not help her with answers, we sent her detailed information on endometriosis and fertility, advised her about an endometriosis support group and an infertility doctor who specializes in endometriosis.

For other women, particularly those whose surgery had occurred due to endometriosis, on-going symptoms (such as bloating and pain) after a hysterectomy and bilateral oophorectomy caused considerable emotional distress and confusion. They participated in the research to find an explanation for their symptoms. Their distress was compounded by a lack of empathy experienced in medical encounters–something which had characterized their earlier health-seeking and which they had thought they would not have to deal with again.

Angie. Following a hysterectomy (for fibroids) and bilateral oophorectomy (for endometriosis), Angie sought medical advice for continuing abdominal pain. Following (third and final) surgery to remove her remaining ovary, her doctor had given her a report stating that endometriosis and adhesions (scar tissue deposits from surgeries) had caused her pain and discomfort. After reading this, she understood that the purpose of her surgeries had been to remove the endometrial growths– thus to relieve the pain–and so found later pain incomprehensible. In addition, the doctor had treated her as if her pain was imagined, and dismissed her complaints. Following an interview, confident that she was supported and her complaints had been heard, Angie attended a hospital casualty department (accompanied by a researcher) where she received information about bowel adhesions and her symptoms. Pain management techniques were explained, and she was referred to a bowel surgeon for on-going care; the emergency physician sent a letter to her local GP. Angie began to manage her pain and abdominal discomfort much better as she knew the cause, and effective self-care strategies.

'Advocacy-Providers'

In contrast to the advocacy-seekers, several women described their roles as informal advocates for other women. 'Advocacy-providers' used their own experiences to actively promote women's health care needs. Several provided advocacy through sharing their experiences. Denise had no informal support during her experiences with endometriosis and infertility; since then, she became an 'advocacy-provider':

> There is nobody in my social network that has been through what I have been through, but I am quite happy and comfortable to talk to [other women] . . . sometimes they'll ring me. One of my very good friends rang me when her daughter started her periods and she said to me, "she has the most painful periods, tell me what it was like for you."

Similarly, difficulties in seeking appropriate health care for endometriosis and dysmenorrhoea led Mandy to her informal health advocate role. She described her passion and commitment to advocating for other women's health care:

> [People] think I'm an absolute mad woman because I want everybody to know everything they possibly could about endometriosis and how the doctors do this, that and the other. And if they say this, you can do that.

After years of struggling with the symptoms of poly-cystic ovarian syndrome, Carolyn found that being an advocacy-provider also benefited the advocate's health:

> What's been terrific is my little network of friends . . . we've done all this investigating and we've talked to other women, and now we use unbleached toilet paper [to stop vulval itching] . . . I don't use soap when I wash my genitals. . . No practitioner ever told me; it was something I discovered through conversation with other women, which has been terrific. So when I heard another friend say "I'm getting urinary tract infection all the time," I said, "hang on, try this." It's amazing how other women have helped me a lot . . . other women's stories.

The advocacy role of some women was not directly related to their own health; rather they had chosen careers in fields that enabled them to advocate for women's health in a broader capacity. Several women had found a way of introducing their support for other women through formal structures, such as working in a health center, health-related government department or as nurses. Although Katrina found health-seeking difficult during her personal experiences with endometriosis, she received quality health care during her treatment, which she attributes to her personal resources and her women's health education. Through her work in a community health service, she was often an advocate for other women experiencing endometriosis:

> Pretty much anyone who rings up about endometriosis or stuff associated with that . . . [the receptionist] will usually put them through to me. So quite often we'll have conversations and then follow up conversations with women.

At the same time, her realization that other women also experienced difficulties receiving quality health care encouraged her to broadly support other women through her work activities:

> Certainly we . . . help women advocate all the time. To get another opinion, to find out more, to persist in whatever it is. It's a huge thing that's needed and so many women give up and they're not supported. They're not supported by their partners, or they might not have friends to bounce ideas off or have to put up with some shitty little male GP, in a little town, because they don't have a car to get to decent place.

Through her work, Katrina initiated changes in women's health seeking behaviors and empowered them to be active decision-makers. She acknowledged the barriers faced by rural women in accessing women-friendly health services, and provided them with the skills to challenge medical professionals when they perceived the need to do so.

Professional support is important when coping with adverse health concerns. For example pregnancy loss is a time when women may feel alone or depressed (Boyce, Condon, & Ellwood, 2002) and benefit from hearing about other women's experiences (Cote-Arsenault & Freije, 2004). Given her complicated obstetric history–of miscarriage, stillborn babies, neonatal deaths and very premature babies–Diane, a nurse, was often sought out by other women with similar issues:

If we have anyone that has miscarriages or if there's [premature] babies around, find me, and that poor mother will know we have something in common. There was a woman who had a 26-weeker, and we were quite friendly for a while. [My daughter] was a lot sicker than this little girl. But it was good that she could know someone that was in a similar situation. And if I can help anyone, it is no skin off my nose.

As with many other informal advocacy-providers, Diane's role was particularly poignant given that she had very limited social support when she had, and lost, her babies. Despite this, her coping strategies during these events enhanced her practice as a health professional:

> ... It [personal pregnancy loss experience] certainly has served me well in my nursing now. I get right in there with all the families and once you're in there, they are ever thankful that you've given them ... strength or understanding of what they're going through.

The role of 'advocacy-provider' was not always straight-forward or unproblematic. Many advocacy-providers did so after their own negative experiences seeking health care or support. The skills and strategies of these women were shared with others who potentially faced the same experiences. Their provision of advocacy derived from their desire for other women to access quality health care and feel empowered in the process.

'Story-Tellers'

Story-telling is an important process for many women, which allows them to challenge dominant and/or hierarchical social structures and discourses (Williams, Labonte, & O'Brien, 2003). In the context of this paper, story-tellers expressed their dissatisfaction with particular health providers or the medical system in general. They wanted their narratives to be used by other women; their role was potential lay-health advocacy.

Fiona. After many years of pain and disruption from endometriosis and seeking advice from a range of medical practitioners, Fiona sought assistance from an alternative health practitioner; since then, she has managed her symptoms through diet control. She described her experiences to us:

I was having quite a few symptoms [and] I knew something wasn't right, and then I went to three different doctors. Luckily, the last doctor I went to, he must have recognized the symptoms and referred me on to a specialist where I had a laparoscopy. But before that, the doctors just said it was depression or they gave it some other name; [they said] "go home and live with it" sort of thing . . . They burnt a lot of the endometrial tissue off. And then I tried a six month treatment with a capsule implant, but the symptoms and side effects of that were pretty horrific, and I didn't really feel any benefits from that. After that, the doctor suggested I could have the surgery [hysterectomy] or try other medication, but I declined that . . . And then I went to a naturopath . . . she actually diagnosed it through tests without me telling her what the problem was . . . she got me on an anti-Candida diet; she said basically before endometriosis comes Candida, which [fitted because] I felt something was wrong with my system all along. And so after changing my diet and having homeopathic drops and medication for eight months, the last test I had with her was it didn't show up, and . . . basically I've got it under control.

Through our dissemination of her story (a research outcome), Fiona hoped other women would become aware of alternatives to allopathic medical explanations of causality and treatment. The majority of participants fell into this category, and neither sought advocacy for their own health nor provided advocacy for other women. Rather, they told their story in the hope that the study outcomes might help other women–thus, their advocacy was indirect. Several themes were raised by 'story-tellers': quality of care; the interconnectedness of physical and emotional health; decision-making; and social isolation. We present these below and discuss their implications for advocacy.

QUALITY OF CARE

Perceptions that their health care was sub-standard or inappropriate prompted the participation of several women. Mija experienced the traumatic birth of her only child twelve years before her interview; following failure to dilate and fetal distress, a forceps delivery was performed which resulted in third-degree (tear through skin, muscle and anal sphincter [RCOG, Adams, & Fernando, 2001]) perineal and cervical tearing. After discussion with family members (also health care professionals), she believed obstetric staff made errors during the delivery and after-care:

> From what I can gather, I wasn't dilated even when she was born. They used forceps in the end. They wouldn't give me an epidural which I called for, for about two hours . . . I had so many stitches in the end. They kept saying to me, "Oh it's nearly here, it's too late [for a caesarean]" and they said that for three hours . . . They just kept saying "no, you don't, the baby's nearly here, you can't use it now." I don't know why, what their excuse was, except maybe it was late Friday night, and it was just before Christmas, and . . . they didn't want to call somebody in . . . The doctor was only there for the last ten minutes anyway.

In the days following the birth, Mija experienced high levels of pain, yet no explanation was offered for what had occurred during the delivery. Her obstetrician was vague, and in response to her question, "How many stitches do I have," he told her "Well, eight's a lot and you had a lot more than that." She felt that the lack of understanding about bodily privacy–"Every nurse that came in, changed shift was sent over to my room to check it [my wound] out. It was quite embarrassing"–reflected a lack of appropriate care. Readmission to the hospital because of an infected wound reinforced Mija's belief that her care was poor. The substandard medical care had far reaching implications–damage to her cervix meant that she was unable to have another child, as she was told that her cervix was too compromised to carry a fetus, and subsequently had surgery to remove her cervix. Since the birth, intercourse has been extremely painful, and her sexual response was significantly impaired, which has affected her relationship with her partner. Her day-to-day bodily comfort was affected by stretching sensations in her vaginal scarring.

INTERCONNECTEDNESS OF PHYSICAL AND EMOTIONAL HEALTH

The physical health of women in this study profoundly impacted on their emotional health status. Over many years of coping with endometriosis, Bronwyn experienced high levels of fatigue and general ill-health:

I ended up with yes, fatigue. I had to get up, get the kids to school, make the beds, wash up, that's the day's work. And I was just so tired. And then I developed a heap of food allergies or sensitivities . . . I couldn't digest things. I'd go to the doctor and they'd take a blood test and they'd say "you're not in menopause. Go away you silly, neurotic woman." Instead of, "you're not in menopause. There's something wrong. Let's look further." But you're so sick you couldn't think. And that was another problem when you don't think properly and you're very emotional. That's very wearing.

The failure of medicine to recognize the intersection of women's emotional and physical health meant that women who presented to their doctor were often dismissed, which frequently resulted in inappropriate treatment–particularly when women were dismissed as over-reacting or being "hysterical" (Cox, Ski, Wood, & Sheahan, 2003). After being dismissed, Bronwyn kept a record of her periods to illustrate to her doctor that, rather than being imagined, her symptoms were real and legitimate:

[Describing her record of her periods] Three weeks, two days, four weeks, four days, two weeks, three weeks, five days, three weeks, three days, two weeks . . .

Through participation in this research, story-tellers were able to gain legitimacy and validation of their experiences. The very process of *not* being dismissed was empowering; through their involvement in the research, they received a form of advocacy–via social support that the researchers provided; Bronwyn was eventually diagnosed with endometriosis.

PATIENT DECISION-MAKING
AND EMPOWERMENT OF WOMEN

In general, women in our study preferred female medical practitioners. However, misdiagnosis or failure to diagnose women appropriately led them to seek a second opinion, regardless of the gender of the provider. For example, Fiona sought treatment from a male GP, who diagnosed her with depression; she then saw a female GP, who similarly diagnosed depression. Only after consulting a third (male) doctor was she referred to a gynecologist who diagnosed her with endometriosis.

Other women described being dismissed by their female provider yet gained quality health care from male providers. Hence, while women initially expected female practitioners to be more sensitive to their health care needs, informed by their own experiences, they modified their health-seeking behavior.

SOCIAL ISOLATION

Social isolation played an important role in the decision of many women to participate. Janice, for example, experienced unexpectedly intense emotional responses to her hysterectomy. Living away from the nearest town, very few people were available with whom she could discuss her dysmenorrhoea and subsequent hysterectomy; she felt very alone despite support from her family and doctor (her only supports). Janice felt that through her participation, other women might become aware of the possible responses to hysterectomy and would therefore be better prepared for adverse outcomes:

> When I saw [the media release], I said to [my husband], "I'm going to do this because I think women should know a bit more about the emotional side of hysterectomy and how it can play with the mind, because it's really affected me." I never thought it would but it did.

Janice experienced menorrhagia since menarche and was diagnosed with endometriosis after difficulties conceiving her second child. Her periods reached the point that she experienced constant leakage of menstrual blood–she would wear up to five 'super'-sized sanitary pads at once; whilst menstruating, she wouldn't leave the house due to constantly needing to change her sanitary products, and became frustrated at increased self-monitoring for leakages. After the birth of her third child, her doctor suggested hysterectomy:

> I spoke to my doctor and I asked him about all the pros and cons . . . I really trusted him. I knew he wouldn't lie to me, and he told me what it was all about, and he said that things can go wrong. He said you might suffer going through menopause earlier . . . I was so frightened, and I thought about canceling [the surgery] when they phoned up and said, you're booked in for such and such a date. I wasn't sure if I could go through with it. I hadn't read any books on

it and I'm glad I didn't because they would have made me change my mind, and I'd still be putting up with my heavy periods today, I think. My doctor didn't give me the things that could possibly happen emotionally.

Janice felt that she received quality health care and appropriate information and did not regret the hysterectomy. However, as she subsequently experienced major depression, Janice wanted to ensure that other women were prepared for this possibility. As with Janice, lack of support was a factor underlying the participation of other 'story-tellers.' Older women in particular described the absence of any social support or understanding during their experiences. Telling their story enabled them to ensure this was not the case for others–through doing so, they expressed their understanding and empathy.

For some women, events that occurred some decades ago remained unresolved emotionally; telling their story was cathartic and assisted their emotional healing. Some acknowledged that community attitudes had changed over the years; others believed that women continued to feel isolated. By sharing their stories, they hoped to alleviate this isolation to some extent.

DISCUSSION

The fundamental goal of health advocacy, as argued by Avery and Bashir (2003), is to share knowledge about maintaining health and avoiding illness, through formal and informal channels. The women who participated in our research all expressed a desire to prevent other women from feeling isolated, as they did. Women's stories largely fit into Carlisle's (2000) framework on health advocacy. In contrast to Carlisle, however, who assumed the presence of a health promotion practitioner, participants without health-related training generated and enacted lay-health advocacy themselves. Representational advocacy is partly missing; women neither relied upon medical evidence, nor sought prevention for their physical health problems–instead, they accepted that these were unavoidable. Relying on their own experiences, they emphasized a desire for doctors and other health professionals to be more responsive when women present with these conditions, thus preventing emotional distress. Advocacy-seekers and some advocacy-providers anticipated that their experiences would evoke structural changes in the medical health care. They assumed that the researchers would use the findings to initiate change–a type of social policy reform–to improve the health outcomes of other women (also described by Avery & Bashir, 2003). Story-tellers perceived themselves as contributing to community activism advocacy–they hoped that participation may enable other women with similar experiences to their own to know that they were not alone. Community development advocacy–helping others with health-related decision-making–was only possible for women employed in health services; most advocacy-providers fell into this category.

In accordance with our findings, Shaw (2002) also argued that, increasingly, lay people are becoming experts (or 'experienced clients'), who take on a pseudo-professional approach to understanding and managing their own health. Through this, patients demonstrated their desires to educate others about the health care options not promoted by health professionals. In that respect, lay-health advocates have published health auto-ethnographies (Broyard, 1992; Frank, 2002), self-help books (Boss, Sterling, & Legro, 2000; Cooke & Trickey, 2002) or established support groups (Gawler, 2001; Whelan, 2003); some of these publications address the reproductive health problems discussed here. Personal health experiences were necessary for being lay-health advocates, as described in this paper.

Our study revealed that health care services can potentially rely on a large pool of people to support patients who lack the health-related knowledge, are unfamiliar with effective coping strategies, and do not have in their informal social networks people who can act as health advocates. The strain on formal health supports can be minimized and the health outcomes for women improved if lay-health advocacy is put into action. Within Australia, the Cancer Council of Victoria's 'Cancer Connect' program illustrates an effective way of incorporating lay-health advocacy into health care practice. Through this program, patients are referred to another patient–a lay advocate–to share their experience with each other and gain support. This simultaneously reduces the load on health care networks and lessens emotional distress. Another benefit of employing lay health advocacy discussed in this paper is its potential cost-effectiveness. Several international studies demonstrate that lay-health advocates trained by health professionals can be effective. For example, Kegler and Malcoe (2004) found that trained lay-health advisors in the United States were effective in preventing adverse health outcomes among children. Meister and colleagues (1992) demonstrated that trained lay-health advocates enhanced prenatal care for low-income Hispanic women. Our study differs somewhat from these as our participants did not necessarily receive any formal advocacy training and did not become advocates through a directed intervention; women themselves initiated the advocacy role. Despite these differences, their narratives suggest that lay-health advocates could be used by health services to enhance emotional health and well-being of patients, across many varied health conditions; further research is required to identify contextually-appropriate strategies to do this.

Limitations. The generalizability of our findings is limited as a self-selected sample was used in the study; the low levels of women from lower socio-economic status, non-English speaking backgrounds, and lesbian and urban women, as well as a high proportion of women with a health education, reflect this. We did not seek to gain a representative sample; instead the study sought to understand the complex issues faced by women with limited social support and, as such, emphasized rural and regional women in recruitment strategies. Despite such limitations, this study provides an insight into how women can support each other informally, outside of formal structures.

NOTE

1. Definition of conditions:

Endometriosis occurs when the uterine lining is found in bodily locations outside the uterus.

Hysterectomy is the surgical removal of the uterus. *Oophorectomy* is the surgical removal of the ovaries.

Common serious disorders of pregnancy include pre-eclampsia (consisting of high blood pressure, increasing levels of protein in the urine, and swelling); fetal growth restriction (when the infant is smaller than expected for its gestational age); placenta previa (when the placenta covers all or part of the cervix); and threatened or actual pre-term labour and delivery.

Unresolved infertility relates to when a woman is unable to conceive, despite continued attempts to do so, either with or without medical intervention.

Early menopause is defined when a woman experiences menopause (cessation of ovarian function) before she is 40 years old.

Poly-cystic ovarian syndrome (PCOS) occurs when there is a hormone imbalance within the ovaries, usually related to an excess of androgen, leading to the development of multiple cysts upon the ovary surface.

Other conditions include breast-feeding failure (when a woman is unable to breast-feed, despite her wish to do so), cervical dysplasia (abnormal cervical cells), and traumatic child-birth.

REFERENCES

Australian Bureau of Statistics (ABS) (1997). *Australian Standard Classification of Occupations. Second edition* (No. 1220.0). Canberra: ABS.

Australian Institute of Health & Welfare (AIHW) (1998). *Health in rural & remote Australia* (Cat. No. PHE 6). Canberra: AIHW.

ATLAS-ti Scientific Software Development (2004). *ATLAS-ti Version 5.0.* Berlin: ATLAS-ti Scientific Software Development.

Avery, B. & Bashir, S. (2003). The road to advocacy–searching for the rainbow. *American Journal of Public Health, 93*:1207-1210.

Block, P., Skeels, S., Keys, C. & Rimmer, J. (2005). Shake-it-up: Health promotion and capacity building for people with spinal cord injuries and related neurological disabilities. *Disability & Rehabilitation, 24*:185-190.

Boss, A., Sterling, E.W. & Legro, R. (2000). *Living with PCOS: Poly-Cystic Ovarian Syndrome.* Omaha: Addicus Books.

Boughton, M.A. (2002). Premature menopause: Multiple disruptions between the woman's biological body experience and her lived body. *Journal of Advanced Nursing, 37*:423-430.

Boyce, P.M., Condon, J.T. & Ellwood, D.A. (2002). Pregnancy loss: A major life event affecting emotional health and well-being. *Medical Journal of Australia, 176*: 250-251.

Brown, W.J., Young, A.F. & Byles, J.E. (1999). Tyranny of distance? The health of mid-age women living in five geographical areas of Australia. *Australian Journal of Rural Health, 7*:148-154.

Broyard, A. (1992). *Intoxicated by my illness and other writings on life and death.* New York: Clarkson Potter.

Burling, L. & Webb, S. (2005). It helped to build me up, knowing that she been there and had got through it herself. *Mental Health Today,* April 18.

Bybee, D.I. & Sullivan, C.M. (2002). The process through which an advocacy intervention resulted in positive change for battered women over time. *American Journal of Community Psychology, 30*:103-132.

Carlisle, S. (2000). Health promotion, advocacy and health inequalities: A conceptual framework. *Health Promotion International, 15*:369-376.

Cooke, K. & Trickey, R. (2002). *Endometriosis: Natural and medical solutions.* Crows Nest: Allen & Unwin.

Cote-Arsenault, D. & Freije, M.M. (2004). Support groups helping women through pregnancies after loss. *Western Journal of Nursing Research, 26*:650-670.

Cox, H., Ski, C.F., Wood, R. & Sheahan, M. (2003). Endometriosis, an unknown entity: The consumer's perspective. *International Journal of Consumer Studies, 27*:200-209.

Frank, A.W. (2002). *At the will of the body: Reflections on illness.* Boston: Mariner Books.

Gawler, I. (2001). *You can conquer cancer: Prevention and management.* Melbourne: Hill of Content.

Glaser, B.G. & Strauss, A.L. (1967). *The discovery of grounded theory: Strategies for qualitative research.* Chicago: Aldine Publishing Co.

Government of Victoria. (2004). Victorian Population Health Survey 2003. Selected findings. Melbourne: Department of Human Services.

Hawe, P. & Shiell, A. (2000). Social capital and health promotion: A review. *Social Science & Medicine, 51*: 871-885.

Kegler, M.C. & Malcoe, L.H. (2004). Results from a lay health advisor intervention to prevent lead poisoning among rural Native American children. *American Journal of Public Health, 94*: 1730.

Kitzinger, C. & Willmott, J. (2002). 'The thief of womanhood': Women's experience of polycystic ovarian syndrome. *Social Science & Medicine, 54*: 349-361.

McFarlane, J. & Wiist, W. (1997). Preventing abuse to pregnant women: Implementation of a "mentor mother" advocacy model. *Journal of Community Health Nursing, 14*: 237-249.

Mead, S., Hilton, D. & Curtis, L. (2001). Peer support: A theoretical perspective. *Psychiatric Rehabilitation Journal, 25*: 134-141.

Mechanic, D. (1999). Issues in promoting health. *Social Science & Medicine, 48*: 711-718.

Meister, J.S., Warrick, L.H., de Zapien, J.G. & Wood, A.H. (1992). Using lay health workers: Case study of a community-based prenatal intervention. *Journal of Community Health, 17*: 37-51.

Palmer, C. (2000). Self-advocacy among people with disabilities in the transition from good will to civil rights: Is it sufficient? *Work, 14*: 61-65.

Paxton, S. (2002). The impact of utilizing HIV-positive speakers in AIDS education. *AIDS Education and Prevention, 14*: 282-294.

Royal College of Obstetrics & Gynaecology (RCOG), Adams, E., & Fernando, R. (2001). RCOG guideline No. 29: *Management of third- and fourth-degree perineal tears during vaginal delivery.* London: RCOG.

Shaw, I. (2002). How lay are lay beliefs? *Health, 6*: 287-299.

SPSS Inc. (2001). *SPSS 11.0 for Windows.* Chicago.

Sullivan, C.M. & Bybee, D.I. (1999). Reducing violence using community-based advocacy for women with abusive partners. *Journal of Consulting & Clinical Psychology, 67*: 43-53.

Whelan, E. (2003). Putting pain to paper: Endometriosis and the documentation of suffering. *Health, 7*: 463-482.

Williams, L., Labonte, R. & O'Brien, M. (2003). Empowering social action through narratives of identity and culture. *Health Promotion International, 18*: 33-40.

Wilson, S.E., Andersen, M.R. & Meischke, H. (2000). Meeting the needs of rural breast cancer survivors: What still needs to be done? *Journal of Women's Health & Gender-Based Medicine, 9*: 667-677.

doi:10.1300/J013v43n04_03

The Culture
of Domestic Violence Advocacy:
Values of Equality/Behaviors of Control

Diana Schow, MA

SUMMARY. Domestic violence advocacy is a culture unto itself. The themes it addresses, in combination with the dominant frames of discourse (Fairclough, 1989) used in the daily conversations of advocates and their supporters, contribute to the stagnation of domestic violence advocacy as a profession and stunt its ability to address the non-homogenous, culturally diverse group of men, women and children living under the tyranny of violence within their homes. Social and political ties to funding institutions and government agencies reify existing concepts about domestic violence education and allow little opportunity for improvement. This article details the methodology and findings of a qualitative, ethnographic research project conducted at an undisclosed domestic violence agency. Qualitative results were analyzed using methods of grounded theory, discourse analysis and narrative analysis. Results revealed four major discourse themes that contribute to the current culture of domestic violence advocacy: (1) systemic contributions to the normalization of crisis, (2) cultural contradictions between paradigms and practice of domestic violence advocacy, (3) ambiguity over the line be-

---

Diana Schow is Adjunct Faculty, Department of Anthropology, Idaho State University, Pocatello, ID 83209 USA (E-mail: campdian@isu.edu).

[Haworth co-indexing entry note]: "The Culture of Domestic Violence Advocacy: Values of Equality/ Behaviors of Control." Schow, Diana. Co-published simultaneously in *Women & Health* (The Haworth Medical Press, an imprint of The Haworth Press, Inc.) Vol. 43, No. 4, 2006, pp. 49-68; and: *Women's Health: New Frontiers in Advocacy & Social Justice Research* (ed: Elizabeth Cartwright, and Pascale Allotey) The Haworth Medical Press, an imprint of The Haworth Press, Inc., 2006, pp. 49-68. Single or multiple copies of this article are available for a fee from The Haworth Document Delivery Service [1-800-HAWORTH, 9:00 a.m. - 5:00 p.m. (EST). E-mail address: docdelivery@haworthpress.com].

tween childhood and adulthood and (4) assumptions about "victim-hood." doi:10.1300/J013v43n04_04 *[Article copies available for a fee from The Haworth Document Delivery Service: 1-800-HAWORTH. E-mail address: <docdelivery@haworthpress.com> Website: <http://www.HaworthPress.com> © 2006 by The Haworth Press, Inc. All rights reserved.]*

KEYWORDS. Domestic violence, advocacy, culture, qualitative, discourse analysis, crisis, victim

BACKGROUND

An extensive amount of research on domestic violence has occurred in the United States within the past 25 years (Dutton, 1998, Ridley and Feldman, 2003, Rothenberg, 2002). Only in recent years have women's studies engaged in research about domestic violence advocates and domestic violence advocacy programs (Carlson & Worden, 2005, O'Sullivan and Carlton, 2001). A review of anthropological literature revealed many studies on domestic violence at individual, social and political levels (Adelman, 2004, Meyer-Emerick, 2002). In relation to discourse styles and behavioral responses to dominant frames of discourse among domestic violence advocates as they interact with their clientele, only one article remotely addressed the topic (Dell, 2000). What was found in the literature was a trend that demonstrates an increase in domestic violence research and advocacy program implementation within the sphere of health care and medicine (Espinoza, 2005, Evans, 2005, Mitchell, 2000).

In the United States, domestic violence advocates are the primary domestic violence educators and service providers. The National Domestic Violence Hotline publishes a list of the network of domestic violence advocacy coalitions from all 50 states. These coalitions supply shelter, education, legal advocacy and case management to people in domestic violence situations (National Domestic Violence Hotline, 2005). In exchange for complying with service provision under the Violence Against Women Act (VAWA), this network, as well as individual organizations within it, receives funding from the Federal Office on Violence Against Women (OVW). This network of domestic violence advocacy programs, in association with its relationship to funding sources, has significant influence on the development of cultural norms within domestic violence advocacy programs.

Many educational materials that are distributed by domestic violence agencies are derived from feminist perspectives. They contain discourse and behavioral recommendations that view a male-dominated, patriarchal society as largely responsible for the existence of domestic violence against women (Cook, 1997, Duluth Model, 2005, Mills, 2003, Walker, .1979). Cook contends that this feminist view has so strongly shaped how domestic violence shelters, education programs, offender programs, and federal and state laws define domestic violence that individuals falling outside of this narrow definition of acceptable domestic violence crime victims have great difficulty receiving assistance (28-35).

Though Cook's critique has validity, as evidenced by the difficulty that lesbian, gay and bi-sexual people have had obtaining equal protection under the law for domestic violence offenses (Peterman and Dixon, 2003), through the feminist approach, much information has come to light about domestic violence and its dynamics, especially within the United States (Dobosh and Dobosh, 1980, Walker, 1979). Cornerstone educational tools such as the Cycle of Violence and the Power and Control Wheel (Duluth Model, 2005, Walker, 1979) have been used to help many people escape violent relationships (Duluth Model, 2005, Egeland et al., 1988). Nonetheless, domestic violence advocacy programs have a responsibility to research how the application of feminist theory has contributed to current cultural norms of domestic violence advocacy. This is especially so in light of the profession's expansion into the health care arena where it is hoped that efforts to reduce domestic violence will have a significant impact.

RESEARCH OBJECTIVES

It is the objective of this research to better understand how the culture of domestic violence advocacy shapes knowledge, attitudes and policy about domestic violence.

Through deconstruction and analysis of discourse and narratives, this study explores the interaction between feminist-based perspectives at a rural United States domestic violence advocacy program, and its hierarchically-structured funding agencies (e.g., OVW). It also explores the influence that the interaction between these organizations has on the ways in which domestic violence education is conceptualized and delivered to clientele (Derrida and Caputo, 1997, Gumperz, 1982), and ultimately on the ways in which cultural values ascribed to by domestic violence advocates reify the system of domestic violence service delivery.

Analyzing narratives and ethnographic accounts of professionals and their clientele reveals the cultural meanings behind commonly used phrases and assumptions about the nature of domestic violence. Existing power structures within the profession of domestic violence advocacy are analyzed to determine whether or not they shape how advocates and their clientele engage in frames of discourse and behaviors associated with domestic violence (Fairclough, 1989, Foucault and Gordon, 1980). Once identified, frames of discourse and behaviors can be concentrated upon for the purpose of improving domestic violence services and policies.

DEFINING TERMS–
ADVOCATES, ANTHROPOLOGISTS AND APHORISMS

Discourse and narrative analysis require a solid definition of terminology used in the methodological process. Three phrases were fundamental to this data analysis and its conclusions: (1) advocacy, (2) domestic violence advocacy and (3) anthropologist as advocate. Advocacy, as the central theme of the study should be understood in its context. Some anthropologists and other professionals refer to advocacy as a behavior that involves *"acting or interceding on behalf of another"* (Encarta, 2005). Kurpius and Rozecki suggest that

> Advocacy may be best defined as a process for pleading the rights of others who for some reason are unable to help themselves to acquire the services, treatment, or both, that they have a right to receive. In this regard, the advocate seeks prevention or remediation for a client group from those who have the power and authority to make the desired changes. (1992)

Prior to conducting interviews, the researcher learned, through casual conversation, that advocates did not assume that clients needed intercession. Advocates spent as much time as possible offering new forms of knowledge and power to clients. This perspective is in line with the ideals of the Duluth Model of domestic violence education (2005), which was used regularly at the studied agency. In this model, clientele were taught about "healthy relationships" that focused on creating *"shared responsibility, balance of power, equality-based decision-making and non-violent negotiation processes"* (2005).

Advocating for persons in domestic violence situations is practiced by many professionals: attorneys, mental health counselors, social workers, psychologists, medical doctors and nurses. Another category of domestic violence professionals is comprised of individuals who work for shelters and who provide case management, resource and referral services, court assistance and domestic violence education. Individuals in this category often identify themselves as "Domestic Violence Advocates." In the United States, the first category of professionals holds academic degrees or certifications in their specific areas of expertise that can only be obtained at institutions of higher education (MDs, RNs, Certified Counselors, etc.). The second category of professionals may or may not hold degrees or certifications. If they do not hold degrees they are considered professionals because they attend trainings within the domestic violence circuit and/or they gain experience through apprenticeship activities. While some of these individuals may have experienced domestic violence themselves, and thereby have a larger understanding of its impact, results of this research indicated that only 3 out of the 20 professionals disclosed such an experience. Many professionals in this category hold a grass-roots perspective and have built services within their own communities based upon a perceived need. It is the second category of professionals with which this research is concerned.

Finally, the researcher for this project is an anthropologist with nine years of experience advocating for individuals and families in domestic violence situations. The controversy over whether anthropologists should be advocating for the organizations or individuals that they study is one that has been explored and critiqued in-depth throughout the last two decades (Beckett, 2004, Hastrup and Elsass, 1990, Scheper-Hughes, 1992). This research project was predicated on the philosophies espoused by those anthropologists who insist upon researching situations in their context, and who do not shy away from advocating for individuals experiencing social and political injustices (Clifford and Marcus, 1986, Scheper-Hughes, 1992, Kleinman, 1986).

METHODS

Participant Recruitment

Research presented in this article represents a subset of secondary findings that was derived from a primary, two-year, qualitative research project conducted at an undisclosed domestic violence agency in a rural United States setting. The primary project included 72 qualitative, semi-structured, open-ended interviews that were conducted with domestic violence advocates and their English and Spanish-speaking clientele. The objective of the primary project was to develop a culturally and linguistically flexible domestic violence curriculum. This primary project was completed in August of 2005. A culturally pliable domestic violence curriculum was developed and presented to the agency and its funding source. Recommendations for a nation-wide pilot test have been made. Advocates at the agency received training and were instructed to use the curriculum.

This article describes the analysis of the secondary findings from that study. These findings were derived from 36 of the 72 primary interviews and were conducted with a total of 34 individuals. The secondary findings shed light on the cultural dynamics of advocacy that shape knowledge, attitudes and policy about domestic violence among advocates and their English-speaking, non-Hispanic clientele. In the secondary data set, 20 of the 34 interviewees were professionals who worked in an advocate capacity for the domestic violence agency. Two of the professionals were interviewed twice, which made the total number of interviews 22. The remaining 14 interviewees were English-speaking, non-Hispanic clientele at the agency who were also observed by the researcher during 52 weeks of domestic violence education groups. English-speaking interviewees not observed during group were excluded from this data set.

Recruitment varied in the study. Professionals working for the agency were required as a part of their jobs to participate in program evaluation and planning. The interviews became a natural part of this process. Informed consent was not required in this instance. Only those professionals who worked directly with persons dealing with domestic violence were approached for interviews. The researcher allowed all professionals who did not want to participate to be excluded from the study. All professionals who worked at the agency and who were directly involved with provision of domestic violence services to individuals or their families were asked to participate. Only two professionals declined to participate out of the twenty-two who were originally invited.

Clientele were recruited at point of contact with the agency. Individuals recruited for participation were those who made their way to the program through existing referral channels (police department, child and family services, hospitals, etc.) or because they were already aware of the agency (prior contact or friends and family).

Eligibility criteria for clientele included individuals who were non-Hispanic, who spoke English, and who were appropriate for receipt of group education services. Hispanic individuals who resided in the area and received services at the agency were predominantly Spanish-speaking. They were excluded from this analysis due to language differences (which often required the presence of a translator) and cultural variations. These criteria ensured that participants went through the same systemic process at the agency. The advocates established eligibility for participation in the group. Upon intake at the agency, if the person was deemed appropriate for group services and the person was non-Hispanic, an advocate would ask them if they would like to participate in the research project. Approximately one-half of those who were queried participated in the study. Participants stayed with the study for varying lengths of time, depending upon their needs and desires for group education services. All participants attended at least one group education session.

A university Human Subjects board approved the study in December of 2003. Informed consent procedures were followed with clientele. The interview process began in January of 2004 and extended through April of 2005.

Data Analysis

All interviews were thematically reviewed using concepts of Grounded Theory, Discourse Analysis and Narrative Analysis.

Grounded Theory, which includes a series of analytical techniques, lends itself to discourse and narrative analysis, as data used in these types of analyses are not easily quantifiable (Glaser, 1978, Jacelon et al. 2005). Such data tend to include stories, detailed accounts of incidents and language frames that vary in their meaning from one user to another. Grounded theory techniques allow researchers to develop theories about data on a case by case basis. Unlike many quantitative approaches, the implementation of Grounded Theory does not assume that an *a priori* theory will explain research results. Instead, it assumes that the data will reveal a theory about a given set of variables after those variables are analyzed in a systematic and reliable manner. Qualitative data, such as open-ended interview responses, must be analyzed in detail to identify contributors to a potential theory. To ensure the integrity of this process all interviews were tape-recorded, transcribed verbatim and analyzed by the researcher for salient themes (McCaslin & Wilson Scott, 2003, Strauss & Corbin, 1990). Topics mentioned more than four times during an interview were considered to be salient themes. Each salient theme was coded and compared to other themes using a side-by-side analysis of the surrounding sections of narrative. Comparison of narratives and codes was also conducted across participant interviews. This process ensured that similar themes were coded the same way from interview to interview. For the purpose of this research, coding of content was based on overt, spoken references to themes. The prevalence of codes signaled common areas of interest, attitudes and beliefs among advocates and their clientele.

Discourse analysis focused on the dynamics of power and social status between speakers (Fairclough, 1989, Gumperz, 1982). Fairclough argued that discourse analysis can reveal how individuals, societies and cultures achieve and maintain levels of power through strategic use of language. In this research the focus of discourse analysis was on a conversational dynamic known as "dominant discourse," which is used to perpetuate power differences (Blommaert & Bulcaen, 2000, Fairclough, 1989). Use of dominant discourse enables interlocuters to control the meanings and uses of words within contextual settings:

> If a discourse so dominates an institution that dominated types are more or less entirely suppressed or contained, then it will cease to be seen as arbitrary, and it will come to be seen as natural and legitimate because it is simply the way of conducting oneself. (1989, 91)

Interview transcripts were reviewed to identify episodes among advocates, their employers and clientele that resulted in power imbalances. These episodes were then compared for similarities and differences. The shared experiences of power imbalance were identified as contributors to the cultural predisposition of the agency.

Narrative Analysis is particularly appropriate for researching a population of individuals who have been exposed to domestic violence (Mills, 2003). When used in analyzing stories and narratives, it allows for the meaning of language and phenomenological experience to vary between individuals (Mills, 2003, 121). This is important to individuals in domestic violence situations whose explanations for their actions are often criticized by close friends and relatives (Walker, 1979). Such criticism marginalizes individuals within their own social groups and leads to stigmatizing assumptions (Goffman, 1963). Narrative analysis was essential to ensuring that the process of Grounded Theory analysis, with its identification of common themes, did not completely overshadow individual experiences. Interview transcripts, group observations and field notes were reviewed to identify markers of individuality that might explain differences of perception among advocates and their clientele.

RESULTS

Overview

The subset of individuals on which this paper focused was largely Caucasian. All of the 14 English-speaking clientele who attended education groups and provided personal interviews were female. Two were Native American and 12 were Caucasian. Of the 20 professionals working at the agency 18 were female and two were male. They self-identified as the following: two were Native American, three were Mexican or Hispanic and 15 were Caucasian. Eighteen were fluent in English. Two were fluent in English and one other language. Five of the fourteen clients completed the entire eight-week domestic violence education group sessions. The remaining nine completed between one and seven weeks of the group sessions. Those who did not complete the group sessions had varying reasons for their decisions. Some did not think it was appropriate for them. Some felt they already knew the material, and some did not like a particular aspect of the group.

A grounded theory approach to data analysis revealed dominant frames of discourse and behavior associated with four themes: (1) systemic contributions to the normalization of crisis, (2) cultural contradictions between paradigms and practice of domestic violence advocacy, (3) ambiguity over the line between childhood and adulthood and (4) assumptions about "victimhood." Each will be discussed individually; however, the concepts are convoluted, and it is an oversimplification to discuss them as completely separate entities. Within this analysis, frames of discourse were identified that substantiated the validity of cultural behaviors that perpetuated staff submissiveness in an environment of control. These behaviors did not harmonize with previously mentioned educational concepts of equality and accountability that were taught to clientele who participated in domestic violence education groups.

Systemic Contributions to the Normalization of Crisis or "Welcome to Non-Profit"

Based on the analysis of the interviews, it was found that three systemic dynamics contributed to crisis existing as a cultural norm in the workplace: (1) adequate access to office space and resources, (2) hierarchical forms of management and (3) perceived demands from funding organizations that limited time. Advocates perceived these dynamics as unchangeable factors that maintained despotic control over work-related activities.

Access to safe office space was in short supply. While conducting this research, part of the agency's ceiling caved in from water damage. The director tried to fix the problem, but it was clearly not the first priority, and no money was available to make repairs. The ceiling was in a long line of other repairs that had to be made. Advocates acknowledged the challenge of the situation and took it in stride as being typical of working for a non-profit agency. During the course of this research, every professional rendered forth some satirical rendition of *"Welcome to non-profit. That's just how things are."*

When space was available, it was frequently described in the interviews as inappropriate. Domestic violence education groups were held at the child-care center. There was no door present to ensure privacy. The center did not have enough child-care providers. The combination of these issues frequently resulted in non-supervised children wandering into the room while group was in session. The children stumbled upon very explicit conversations (many involving explicit details of sexual, physical and emotional abuse). Though it was standard practice at the agency to teach clientele about the traumatic impact that witnessing domestic violence can have on children, and how desensitization results in acceptance of violence within family and community cultures, very little was done to prevent children from entering the group education room. After six months of observing this dynamic, the group facilitator mentioned that the lack of a door was a problem, but said *"We're non-profit and don't have money for a door."*

The second systemic factor that perpetuated crisis was the agency's pyramid-shaped, hierarchical management structure, which enforced social and professional cultural norms of power imbalance that were contradictory to the cultural norms of equality that advocates taught to their clientele (Blanchard et al., 1999). The physical spaces within which advocates worked relegated them to subservience. Executives and program directors had offices on the upper level of the office building while the entire advocate staff had their offices in the basement, which was dark, poorly lit, cold, and very inappropriate for purposes of client confidentiality.

The walls are thin. I can't even close my door properly. Sometimes I just hope no one can hear what's going on. (PI06-advocate)

Advocates discussed frustration with authority figures in the agency who controlled access to important resources like locked filing cabinets.

When someone in staff or on the service provider end, makes recommendations to the administrative end, they either end up getting burnt, ignored or in trouble, and it seems to create more conflict than resolution. (PI02-advocate)

Advocates were not only physically, but socially removed from authority figures.

I don't think I've met all the board of directors, and I think that's kind of hard because they make a lot of decisions about what is and what is not . . . I have three supervisors, so seeing that these three don't communicate real well, and that I'm involved in two different programs, that makes it hard to know what to do and what to expect. (PI05-advocate)

The third influencing factor, funding requirements, like reporting and re-submission of grants, kept advocates so busy that they did not spend sufficient time with clientele.

A lot of the time we're coming up with ways to record and it's taking so long to count those statistics and the recording of them that we're losing time by too much data collection. (PI07-advocate)

I always say you could get so much work done if you didn't have to prove it (PI04). They (funders) forget that in a small rural community it's hard to get numbers numbers numbers. We can't go knocking on doors and saying, you know, 'Are you getting abused?' So, it's just that, in that sense, kind of getting back into knowing what you actually started an agency for. (PI01-advocate)

Money is a big issue to provide stability. It's very unsettling for most staff to know that if a certain grant does not get funded again, "I might not have a job" or it may only be 10 hours a week, and they have a family you know, and if they're not full time they don't get health benefits. So, you know, being able to offer staff long-term stability to provide the services that they provide I think is a big issue. I don't like feeling like I can't promise my staff that they're gonna have jobs from year to year. (PI12-advocate)

This condition is similar to what Chris Argyris, an organizational researcher, described:

We will tend to find that, on the average, due to the organizational structure, managerial controls, and directive leadership, the gap or conflict between the individual's needs and the organizational requirements tends to become worse as one goes down the chain of command and as the job exerts more control over the individual. (p. 41, 1964)

Cultural Contradictions Between Paradigms and Practice of Domestic Violence Advocacy

Narrative analysis, interviews and field observations revealed that advocates engaged in cultural behaviors that if displayed by clientele, would be associated with "victimization issues." Just like victims of domestic violence, advocates surreptitiously criticized the authority that was exerting unfair power and control. They left and returned to that authority, and they resigned themselves to a lack of equality-based decision-making. This resignation reified existing power imbalances among agency staff.

Of the 20 professionals interviewed between January 2003 and January 2005, only seven remained working with the agency at the end of the study period. Two left due to completion of projects, and 11 left for personal or work-related issues. Of these 20 professionals, three left the agency and returned to work there at some point in time, and all but three of them changed work positions within the agency. Of the 8 advocates that provided case-management services between July 2004 and January 2005, six still work with the agency. Two of those six quit and then returned during the research. These figures represent an overall turnover rate of 65%.

The eight advocates running education groups discussed frustration at their lack of training. Four of the eight reported having less than four 2-hour observation sessions before having to run their own client groups:

I'm supposed to run group. I sure hope I'm doing it right. (PI04-advocate)

The facilitator came late to education groups at least 25% of the time. The consensus among advocates was that doing things in a frantic and unprepared manner is something one gets used to. If advocates complained, they were characterized as poor "multi-taskers."

> We do a lot of crisis work and sometimes we have to stop what we're doing and do something else, and we have to multi-task . . . I would like to say that the office runs, you know, things are, you know, "This is how it is and you never have to work outside your job description." But sometimes that doesn't happen . . . we all have to be willing to shift a little bit and adjust and you know, and handle it. (PI03-advocate)

Each of the 8 advocates who provided case management services were also responsible for being on-call between 8 and 30 nights per month. They had to carry the "crisis-line" cell phone with them at all times on these days.

> I guess I thrive on crisis . . . that call in the middle of the night where you know you just gotta go and you know you're going to do something good for the community. (PI06-advocate)

More than one advocate was aware that the agency was not operating in the optimal behavior pattern associated with calmness and equality-based decision-making:

> I have to be careful how I approach (name) because I'm afraid she's gonna run out you know, and want to do it Right Now! You know? And *they'll* know that this is something–communication to be able to get it on the table to be discussed without making a crisis of it. (PI21-advocate)

In the end, as one advocate put it, everything that happened in the agency affected how it served as an equality-based, cultural model for clientele:

> If we can't identify a crisis, how the hell are we gonna teach people how to deal with one? (PI09-advocate)

Ambiguity Over the Line Between Childhood and Adulthood

The fourteen participants from the client group had a total of 34 children. Five out of the fourteen families (36%) had past or present open cases with child protection services.

Many women sought services because of the impact that domestic violence was having on their children. Mothers stated that they were beginning to *"take things out"* on their children:

> I'd get frustrated with [child's name] and I'd get really angry and I didn't know what to do. (CGNPRE08-client)

> His [my father's] mentality of it is you know, I'm a F'n B, you know? Whatever. "You're a slut. You have a bastard child," and, you know, my son's 15 months old. He needs, he is now getting to that point where he understands. You know he sees adult relationships. He sees interactions. He understands that, and I don't want him to grow up with it. (CGNPRE02-client)

Advocates expressed a great deal of concern for both mothers and their children:

> I want to take my clients home, and I want to take their babies home, and that, it's hard for me. (PI09-advocate)

> I think, "Uh!!!! The chance of him killing you is so likely. And with the babies!" (PI09) "That's what made me cry. Watching the babies. . . That in itself is just nothing you would ever want a child to experience or go through. I think when I can't leave it at work it's because children are involved." (PI06-advocate)

Everyone who was interviewed was very concerned about the children. For the mothers, however, it did not matter what age a child was. Two mothers had 17-year-old sons about whom they were very worried. Fortunately, for both these mothers and their sons, they did not need to stay at the shelter. The agency had a policy that boys over the age of thirteen were not allowed to stay in shelter with their mothers. Funding requirements and feminist-based philosophies about the physical and sexual threat posed by young boys were the primary reasons for this policy (Anderson, 1997, Kalmuss, 1984). The agency received a large amount of funding from the Office of Violence Against Women

(OVW). The OVW overwhelmingly supported efforts that focused on reducing violence against women (Department of Justice, 2005):

> Our mission is to provide national leadership in developing the nation's capacity to reduce violence against women through the implementation of VAWA. Our ultimate goal is to change perceptions around violence against women so that these crimes are considered unacceptable and no longer tolerated in our society. (2005)

Due to this focus, and the dearth of reference to services for men in both the 1994 and 2000 versions of VAWA (Violence Against Women Act, 2000), the agency under study came to understand that funding they received from VAWA should not be used to assist male victims. This understanding left them in a dilemma regarding the ambiguity surrounding the exact age when a young boy became an adult male and the companion assumption that he would most likely be a batterer or sexual perpetrator. The result of this contention was manifested in an agency policy that did not equitably provide domestic violence services to all clientele.

Assumptions About "Victimhood"

Eleven of the fourteen (79%) group participants described either themselves or their mothers engaging in an activity that resulted in the victimization of adult males.

> Well with their dad I loved him with all my heart and when things got to a point where the verbal abuse had taken, you know, instead of just being nice to each other we'd say ugly things. Once we started saying ugly things to each other, and the pain and the hurt started to dig in deep, then we started to hit each other. I think that most of the reason that I was violent was because I wanted him to hurt as much as I did, and if I couldn't hurt him emotionally, I was gonna, I was gonna brutalize him physically and make him feel pain one way or another. (CGNPRE06-client)

Eight (57%) of the fourteen clients stated they had taken or needed to take anger management to control their own "*anger, rage and tantrums.*"

> At least I didn't throw nothing or break it because that's what I used to do when I would get mad. And I didn't throw my phone

cause one of my phones, I had to replace it because I threw it. I don't do that anymore. (CGNPOST08-client)

Contrary to these accounts, an example of the agency's cultural perspective that women are the main victims of domestic violence is reified on a poster hanging in the hallway. This poster depicted a woman with red stitches in her face that had the same pattern as the stitches in a baseball. The picture's caption read, *"Don't Slugher."*

Another reification of this stereotype was witnessed during the domestic violence education groups. All four facilitators handed out gender-specific educational materials with a rendition of the following verbal disclaimer:

> I know these papers all say 'she' when they talk about victims, but men can be victims too, but most of them are women. Statistics say only 4-7% of victims are men. (FAC1-group facilitator observed)

If women admitted being abusive, many advocates and two group facilitators responded with statements like, *"You probably did it in self defense."* (FAC 3: group facilitator observed)

DISCUSSION

Examples of systemic contributions to the normalization of crisis and cultural contradictions between philosophies held by funding sources and philosophies held by feminist-minded advocates required advocates to negotiate conflicting obligations associated with an agency that simultaneously: (1) espoused the importance of calm, equality-based, mutually-accountable relationships as the only relationships that are truly non-violent and (2) insisted that the agency's staff must be comfortable with abrupt changes in plan and rule, hierarchical decision-making, and inconsistent measures of accountability. This latter, hegemonic perspective resulted in a stratified hierarchy that dismissed guiding educational principles and adopted authoritative behaviors that required consent and submission from advocates (Gramsci and Forgacs, 2000). This observation is consistent with opinions held by Argyris:

> The formal organization (which includes technology) and the administrative control system typically used in complex formal organizations may be viewed as part of a grand strategy to organize

human effort to achieve specific objectives . . . The strategy creates a complex of organizational demands that tend to require individuals to experience dependence and submissiveness and to utilize few of their relatively peripheral abilities. (58)

While the Violence Against Women Act had been extremely important to the safety of women and children who have suffered under the tyranny of abuse, perceptions of its requirements regarding services to men limited the agency's ability to address the needs of boys between the ages of thirteen and eighteen.

Policy and legislation about qualifying for victim status were fraught with long-held, feminist-based assumptions about sexual predispositions toward violence:

In 92% of all domestic violence incidents, crimes are committed by men against women. *Violence Against Women, Bureau of Justice Statistics, U.S. Department of Justice, January, 1994* (National Domestic Violence Hotline, 2005)

These assumptions reified outdated cultural aspects of domestic violence advocacy, even though research has suggested that women are abusive at a much higher rate than 8% (Cook, 1997, Paradise, 2002). Strauss and Gelles' work states that women are primary aggressors in as many as 35% of domestic violence incidents (1980, 1986). Results from this research, although not statistically significant, indicated an even higher percentage (79%).

This research had limitations. First, we analyzed only one non-randomly selected domestic violence advocacy program in the United States. Thus, the findings presented here may not be considered representative of all such agencies. The sample of participants in the group education process was small so that quantitatively significant results were not obtained. Also, the researcher had worked with family and domestic violence for nine years. It is possible that this prior experience influenced the interpretation of narratives and observations.

Nonetheless, this research is important to the process of understanding how the culture of domestic violence advocacy, with its assumptions and perceptions, reifies who does and does not receive, qualify for and benefit from services. The discourse of advocates and their clientele shed significant light on the attitudes and values that shaped the provision of advocacy services. It also shed light on the individual experiences of clientele. They were more than willing to discuss their own violent behavior in interviews with the researcher. It was not until educational information interceded, such as statistics that purport an extremely low number of female perpetrators, that these discussions dwindled.

Current trends are situating domestic violence advocacy within the health care arena. It is worth evaluating the process by which this occurs. Do health care professionals, as well as all domestic violence professionals, want to receive funding that focuses mainly on supporting services for female victims? Do they want to do something to improve the way services are offered to boys between the ages of 12 and 18? Future research in these areas may lay a path for the emergence of a better form of domestic violence advocacy.

REFERENCES

Adelman, M. 2004. A Model for Teaching an Interdisciplinary Course on Domestic Violence. PoLAR: Political and Legal Anthropology Review, Vol. 27, No. 2: 154-162.

Anderson, K.L. 1997. Gender, status and domestic violence: An integration of feminist and family violence approaches. Journal of Marriage and the Family. 59: 655-669.

Argyris, C., 1964. Integrating the individual and the organization. New York: Wiley & Sons.

Beckett, J. 2004. ATSIC and Beyond: Anthropology, Advocacy and Beauracracy. Soap.

Blanchard, K., Zigarmi, D., & Zigarmi, P. 1999. Leadership and the One Minute Manager: Increasing Effectiveness Through Situational Leadership. William Morrow.

Blommaert, J., & Bulcaen, C. 2000. Critical Discourse Analysis. Annual Review of Anthropology, Vol. 29, pp. 447-466.

Burt, M., Newmark, L., Norris, M., Dyer, D., & Harrell, A. 1994. The Violence Against Women Act of 1994 Evaluation of the STOP Block Grants to Combat Violence Against Women, Program on Law and Behavior, The Urban Institute Uploaded October 2005, *http://www.urban.org/UploadedPDF/vaw-act.pdf*.

Carlson, B.E., & Worden, A.P. 2005. Attitudes and Beliefs About Domestic Violence: Results of a Public Opinion Survey. Journal of Interpersonal Violence, Vol. 20, No. 10.

Cook, P. 1997. Abused Men. The Hidden Side of Domestic Violence. Praeger Publishers.

Clifford, J., & Marcus, G.E. 1986. Writing Culture: The Poetics and Politics of Ethnography. University of California Press.

Dell, P. 2000. Accounting for Domestic Violence: A Q Methodological Study. Violence Against Women, Vol. 6, No. 3, pp. 286-310, Sage Publications.

Derrida, J., & Caputo, J. (Editor). 1997. Deconstruction in a Nutshell: A Conversation With Jacques Derrida (Perspectives in Continental Philosophy): Fordham University Press.

Dobosh, R. E., & Dobosh, R. P. 1980. Violence Against Wives: A Case Against Patriarchy. Shepton Mallet, Somerset: Open Books.

Dutton, D. 1998. The abusive personality: Violence and control in intimate relationships. New York: Guilford Press.

Duluth Model. 2005. Minnesota Program Development Inc. *http://www.duluth-model.org/*.

Egeland, B., Jacobvitz, D., & Sroufe, L. 1988. Breaking the Cycle of Abuse. Child Development, Vol. 59, Issue 4, p. 1080, 9p.

Encarta World English Dictionary. 2005. *http://encarta.msn.com/dictionary_1861583864/advocate.html*.

Espinoza, H. 2005. A paradigm for developing a comprehensive treatment protocol for survivors of domestic violence. Rev Panam Salud Publica. 17(2):116-8.

Evans N. 2005. Domestic violence: Recognizing the signs. Paediatric Nursing. 17(1): 14-6.

Fairclough, N. 1989. Language and Power. England: Longman Group.

Foucault, M. & Gordon, C. (Editor). 1980. Power/Knowledge: Selected Interviews & Other Writings 1972-1977. New York: Pantheon Books.

Glaser B. 1978. Theoretical Sensitivity: Advances in Methodology of Grounded Theory. Sociology Press.

Goffman, E. 1963. Stigma. Notes on the Management of Spoiled Identity. Englewood Cliffs, NJ: Prentice-Hall.

Gramsci, A., & Forgacs, D. (Editor). 2000. The Antonion Gramsci Reader: Selected writings 1916-1935. New York University Press.

Gray, A. 1990. On Anthropological Advocacy. Current Anthropology, Vol. 31, No. 4.

Gumperz, J. 1982. Discourse Strategies. Cambridge University Press.

Hastrup, K. & Elsass, P. 1990. Anthropological advocacy: A contradiction in terms? Current Anthropology. 31(3): 301-311.

Jacelon, C. S., & O'Dell, K. K. 2005. Case and Grounded Theory as Qualitative Research Methods. Urologic Nursing, Vol. 25, Issue 1, p. 49, 4p.

Kalmuss, D. 1984. The intergenerational transmission of marital aggression. Journal of Marriage and the Family. 46, 11-19.

Kleinman, A. 1986. The Illness Narratives: Suffering, Healing and the Human Condition. New York: Basic Books, Inc.

Kurpius, D.J., & Rozecki, T. 1992. Outreach, advocacy, and consultation: A framework for prevention and intervention. Elementary School Guidance and Counseling, 26, 176-189.

McCaslin, M., & Wilson Scott, K. 2003. The Five-Question Method For Framing A Qualitative Research Study, The Qualitative Report, Vol. 8, No. 3, pp. 447-461.

Mills, L. 2003. Insult to Injury: Rethinking Our Responses to Intimate Abuse. Princeton University Press.

Mitchell, C. 2000. National Conference on Health Care and Domestic Violence Plenary Session #2: Moving Towards Evidence-Based Care for Domestic Violence.

Meyer-Emerick, N. 2002. Policy Makers, Practitioners, Citizens: Perceptions of the Violence Against Women Act of 1994, Administration Society; 33: 629-663.

National Domestic Violence Hotline. 2005. *http://www.ndvh.org/*.

O'Sullvian, E., & Carlton, A. 2001. Victim Services, Community Outreach, and Contemporary Rape Crisis Centers: A Comparison of Independent and Multiservice Centers, Journal of Interpersonal Violence, 16: 343-360.

Peterman, L. M., & Dixon, C. G. 2003. Domestic Violence Between Same-Sex Partners: Implications for Counseling. Journal of Counseling & Development, Vol. 81, Issue 1, p. 40, 8p.

Ridley C. A., & Feldman, C. M. 2003. Female Domestic Violence Toward Male Partners: Exploring Conflict Responses and Outcomes. Journal of Family Violence, Vol. 18, No. 3.

Rothenberg, B. 2002. The Success of Battered Woman Syndrome: An Analysis of How Cultural Arguments Succeed. Sociological Forum, Vol. 17, No. 1.

Scheper-Hughes, N. 1992. Death Without Weeping: The Violence of Everyday Life in Brazil, University of California Press.

Strauss, A., & Corbin J. M. 1990. Basics of Qualitative Research Grounded Theory Procedures and Techniques.

Straus, M. A., & Gelles, R. J. 1980. Behind Closed Doors: Violence in the American Family. Doubleday.

Straus, M. A., & Gelles, R. J. 1986. Societal Change and Change in Family Violence from 1975 to 1985 as Revealed by Two National Surveys. Journal of Marriage and the Family. 48. 467.

Violence Against Women Act. 2000 . *http://www.ojp.usdoj.gov/vawo/about.htm.*

Walker, L. 1979. The Battered Woman. Harpercollins.

doi:10.1300/J013v43n04_04

Cervical Cancer Services for Indigenous Women: Advocacy, Community-Based Research and Policy Change in Australia

Lenore Manderson, BA, PhD, FASSA
Elizabeth Hoban, BA, MTH, PhD

SUMMARY. Collaborative research undertaken in the state of Queensland, Australia, resulted in major changes in cervical cancer screening and treatment for Indigenous women. Guided by an Indigenous statewide reference group and with an Indigenous researcher playing a lead role, qualitative data were collected using interviews, focus groups, and larger community meetings; and case studies were conducted with health workers and community members from diverse rural, remote and urban communities, to explore the different cultural and structural fac-

Lenore Manderson is affiliated with the School of Psychology, Psychiatry and Psychological Medicine, Monash University, Caulfield Campus, 900 Dandenong Road, Caulfield East, Victoria 3145, Australia (E-mail: lenore.manderson@med.monash. edu.au). Elizabeth Hoban is affiliated with the School of Health and Social Development, Faculty of Health and Behavioural Sciences, Deakin University, Burwood, Victoria 3125, Australia (E-mail: elizabeth.hoban@deakin.edu.au or lizhob@yahoo.com).

This paper is dedicated to the memory of Maureen Kirk, the Indigenous woman who conceptualized the research on which this paper is based, drove the research, carried it into practice, and inspired us all.

[Haworth co-indexing entry note]: "Cervical Cancer Services for Indigenous Women: Advocacy, Community-Based Research and Policy Change in Australia." Manderson, Lenore, and Elizabeth Hoban. Co-published simultaneously in *Women & Health* (The Haworth Medical Press, an imprint of The Haworth Press, Inc.) Vol. 43, No. 4, 2006, pp. 69-88; and: *Women's Health: New Frontiers in Advocacy & Social Justice Research* (ed: Elizabeth Cartwright, and Pascale Allotey) The Haworth Medical Press, an imprint of The Haworth Press, Inc., 2006, pp. 69-88. Single or multiple copies of this article are available for a fee from The Haworth Document Delivery Service [1-800-HAWORTH, 9:00 a.m. - 5:00 p.m. (EST). E-mail address: docdelivery@haworthpress.com].

tors affecting understanding and awareness of cervical cancer and Indigenous women's use of and access to health services for screening, diagnosis and treatment. These data were supplemented by an analysis of clinical data and health service checklists. We discuss the methodology and summarize the key social and structural factors that discourage women from presenting for screening or returning for follow-up. These include women's misunderstanding of cervical cancer screening, fear of cancer, distrust of health services, poor recall and follow-up systems, and the economic and social burden to women presenting for treatment. We describe how the research process and subsequent activities provided Indigenous women with a vehicle for their own advocacy, resulting in important policy and program changes. doi:10.1300/J013v43n04_05 *[Article copies available for a fee from The Haworth Document Delivery Service: 1-800-HAWORTH. E-mail address: <docdelivery@haworthpress.com> Website: <http://www. HaworthPress.com> © 2006 by The Haworth Press, Inc. All rights reserved.]*

KEYWORDS. Australia, advocacy, cervical cancer, Indigenous health, research ethics

Applied anthropologists have long worked to ensure strong community participation to define research questions and collect, use and control data, reflecting respect in local knowledge of problems, priorities and solutions (Schensul and Stern, 1985; Stull and Schensul, 1987; Lamphere, 2004). Researchers working with Indigenous communities in Canada, the United States, New Zealand and Australia, for example, have long been aware of the need to work with community members to ensure that their work is relevant to policies and programs (Chrisman et al., 1999; Lamphere, 2004; de Souza, 2004). While conventionally the partnerships have been between researchers and the communities they study, partnerships increasingly also include policy makers and service providers to maximize the impact of the research (Minkler and Wallerstein, 2003; Austin, 2004; Singer et al., 2005). Such collaboration, involving participatory research, aims to develop equitable relationships among participants, to ensure appropriate and effective dissemination of findings and consequent action.

In Australia, Indigenous ownership of research is imperative (Australia, 1991; Aboriginal Coordinating Council, 1995). But how this proceeds, in ways that ensure ownership of the findings by both community members and government agencies to effect change, have been less well described. In this paper, we describe the research partnerships and community collaboration in a study of cervical cancer screening, conducted in the northeast state of Queensland, where 30 percent of Indigenous Australians reside. We focus on how, through advocacy and dissemination, the research enhanced official understanding of the social, cultural and historical context that produces poor health outcomes for Indigenous Australians, and how this led to short-term and long-term changes in state government responses to services for Indigenous women and the support of Indigenous health workers.

BACKGROUND

Although program initiatives date from the 1970s, the first major policy commitment to maintain and improve women's health and well-being was the *National Women's Health Policy* (Australia, 1989). In this document, the translation of policy to practice was tied to a re-orientation within the national and state health systems to be more responsive to the women's expressed needs. The document set the stage for changes in health services through the 1990s and subsequently, including for Indigenous and other minority women whose health status was especially poor. States and territories followed this federal initiative, including with respect to cervical and breast cancer. In the northeast state of Queensland, where the research we report here was conducted, Indigenous women, rural and remote women and "high risk" young women were identified as priority groups (Queensland Health, 1993). The Indigenous women included mainland Aboriginal women resident throughout the state and Torres Strait Island women living on the islands of the far north of the state or in coastal areas of the mainland. Concurrently, Indigenous health policies and programs reflected state concern about the continuing health discrepancies of Indigenous and other Australians (Queensland Health, 1992, 1994, 1998a, 1998b). These policies pertaining to Indigenous Australians and all women provided a platform for advocacy and subsequent action.

Cancer is a major cause of Indigenous mortality in Australia, exceeded only by circulatory and respiratory diseases. Queensland Cancer Registry data for 1982-1996 indicate that the age standardized incidence of cervical cancer among Indigenous women was 4.7 times the state average and the mortality rate 13.4 times the state average (Coory et al., 2000). Indigenous women are eleven times more likely than non-Indigenous women to be hospitalized for conditions of the cervix, and ten times more likely to die of cervical cancer than other women in Queensland (four times, Australia wide). High hospitalization rates for women in rural, remote and urban areas suggest that infrastructure is not the sole reason for late presentation. In Australia, cervical cancer screening is available to all women through Medicare, with biannual examination recommended from onset of sexual activity until age 70. Low participation in screening is believed to be a major factor in the mortality rates of Indigenous women. Data from the Queensland Health Pap Smear Registry for 1999-2001 suggest a screening participation percentage in select Indigenous communities that was 30% less than for the rest of the state (Coory, 2002); the disproportionate diagnosis of advanced disease among Indigenous people in the Northern Territory has also been related to poor screening participation rates (Condon et al., 2005). In this paper, we describe our involvement in Indigenous women's health and in particular, cervical cancer screening. We focus on the advocacy that occurred in collaborating with Indigenous women and government officers, both in conducting the research and translating the findings into government policy and programs.

METHODS

In 1997, the Women's Cancer Screening Unit in the Queensland Department of Health (hereafter Queensland Health) commissioned research to improve outcomes for Indigenous women. A central principle of advocacy-based research is that the affected community (or communities) identifies the research question and drives the theoretical and methodological framework and research process (Phillips, 2003; Ishtar, 2005a, 2005b). In this case, the study, *Barriers to and Appropriate Delivery Systems for Cervical Cancer Screening Services in Indigenous Communities in Queensland*, was instigated by and conducted with Maureen Kirk, an Indigenous Australian woman with personal experience of breast cancer. Kirk (1993; Kirk et al., 1995) had already identified the need for this research: it was what she referred to as a "dream" that she wished to see fulfilled–to know why the mortality rate from cancer among Indigenous women was so much greater than for other Australian women.

When the study was commissioned, Kirk was employed as the first Indigenous Cancer Support Officer for Aboriginal and Torres Strait Islander women at the Royal Women's Hospital in Brisbane; for several years previously she had been a volunteer with the Queensland Cancer

Council, the first Indigenous woman so involved. Sufficient funds were allocated within the research budget to enable her to transfer to work full-time as a researcher in the study. Kirk worked with three non-Indigenous Australians from The University of Queensland (including the authors of this paper) (Kirk et al., 1998a), who she had approached for this purpose two years earlier. Six other Indigenous women participated, on the invitation of Kirk, in a state-wide reference group; they included Indigenous health workers and other women who had previous committee experience and were respected for their public views on Indigenous rights. Reference group members provided support and advice to the researchers, and advocated for the project with government and non-government agencies, zonal networks of health workers, Queensland Health and existing local Indigenous women's groups (see also Manderson et al., 1998). Eleven Indigenous women in the study sites participated as members of local community liaison groups and facilitated our research by brokering our entry into their own communities, and identifying and recruiting other women and men to participate in the project. Their involvement was critical: Indigenous Australian communities have clear protocols in relation to researchers; these vary from one community to another. Throughout the study period and subsequently, we regularly consulted with members of the state reference and local liaison groups via teleconferencing, phone and fax, and through face-to-face meetings; we provided them with lengthy verbal summaries of research activities and findings, clarified interpretation, and rehearsed possible recommendations. Kirk's lead role as a researcher was evidence to other women, including those who participated in the study, of the genuineness of the non-Indigenous researchers. The state reference and local liaison groups provided the mechanisms for shared objectives and transparency.

Community consultations regarding the research protocol occurred in October and November 1995, and June to September 1996, with sufficient time to ensure Indigenous women's support. Over the next 12 months, funding agencies were approached, the protocol and budget shaped to accommodate their interests, and ethics approval gained from The University of Queensland Behavioural and Social Sciences Ethical Review Committee. The first trade-off was to substitute cervical for breast cancer: breast cancer, reflecting Kirk's own experience, was not considered a government priority. While cervical cancer was also not a priority of the state health department, national cervical cancer screening strategies, the existence of the Women's Cancer Screening Unit, and the disproportionately high rate of cervical cancer among Indigenous women, provided a rationale and leverage to negotiate the funds to conduct the commissioned research.

Sampling and Recruitment

The objectives were to identify barriers to cervical cancer screening for Indigenous women, recommend appropriate strategies to improve educational and clinical services, compare and contrast models of health service delivery in Queensland and other states, and develop guidelines for a code of best practice in the delivery of services. Women were recruited from four jurisdictional divisions of the state to ensure differences in geographic location, range and type of health services, and composition and size of the local population. The areas included coastal north Queensland and the Torres Strait Islands (administratively part of the state of Queensland), which included the regional capital city of Cairns, to which all serious cases of illness and treatment are referred for medical attention, and remote areas where both mainland Aboriginal and Torres Strait Island women reside. The three other study areas were ones where the Indigenous population is predominantly Aboriginal: remote far northwest Queensland and its coastal administrative and medical referral center, Townsville; and rural southwest Queensland and urban southeast Queensland, for both of which the referral center for tertiary medical care is the state capital, Brisbane. Available rates of cervical cancer, based on hospital and community health service outpatient data, suggested that these were also areas with a strong probability of identifying women already diagnosed with, and treated for, cervical cancer. This sampling method ensured that we included communities theoretically within commuting distance from the major tertiary hospital, and others, including island settlements, which required women to use various means of transport to access treatment centers.

Letters were sent to community councils in select urban, rural and remote communities to seek their willingness for us to visit the community and invite individuals to participate in the study, and women working with us as local liaison members scheduled our visits to the community. Budgetary restrictions to an extent shaped our sampling strategy, preventing state-wide recruitment, but at the same time, purposive sampling ensured diversity. We aimed to recruit as many women as possible through advertisements in local newspapers and their attendance at meetings, organized by local liaison women. Any woman from the study communities who indicated her wish to participate was included in the study, in line with the view of the reference group that all women had something to contribute. Self-nomination to participate was supplemented by personal approaches by local liaison women, to ensure diversity by age: both adolescent and young women, and women who were no longer married or reproductive, tended to link cancer screening to sexual activity and childbearing and assumed they would not be appropriate respondents.

Data Collection

Visits to study communities, from May 1997 to February 1998, were timed on the advice of the community liaison women to avoid ceremonies, other community activities, and infelicitous weather that might affect access. Qualitative research methods were used for data collection, reflecting Indigenous community resistance to standard medical research methodologies (Eades et al., 1999; Panaretto et al., 2003; Ishtar, 2005a, 2005b) and the desire of members of the state reference group and local community women to ensure that their views were elicited in an acceptable manner. Potential participants were provided with Plain Language Statements. Consent forms were developed and approved by the state reference group, and all interviews and focus group participants gave written consent. Confidentiality was carefully maintained during fieldwork. While some people welcomed the opportunity to talk about their experiences, the discussions also raised difficult and emotionally demanding stories, both personal and related to racism experienced within the health system. This highlighted the importance that the research be translated to ensure improved communication, culturally appropriate service provision and increased access to services.

Data were collected from focus group discussions (313 community women, 106 health workers), in-depth interviews (45 community men and women, 73 health workers) and case histories (10 women) while the researchers were resident in the study communities. Extrapolating from government estimates (Australian Bureau of Statistics, 2006), this suggests that around one percent of all Indigenous women resident in Queensland were interviewed. The primary means of assessing veracity and reliability of data, however, derive not from the numbers of women who participated in interviews or focus groups, but from feedback from the reference group and participants at community meetings. Our approach to reliability, representativeness and validity, therefore, was consistent with an ethnographic rather than an epidemiological approach.

Questionnaires and structured interview guides were not considered acceptable. Instead a simple guideline for discussion was used to explore

Indigenous concepts of health and illness, how these concepts affected women's interpretations of screening practices, signs and symptoms of disease, and experiences of treatment. As indicated, participants were not strictly targeted; rather, all women were invited to participate, whether or not they had had cancer. Women with personal experience provided varied accounts of screening, diagnosis, follow-up and treatment, from simple treatment provided by a general practitioner to chemotherapy and radiotherapy at tertiary hospitals. We also explored women's perceptions of health providers and the relevance of this to their participation in screening and adherence to treatment. In-depth interviews were conducted with women who had had abnormal smears, had been treated for or currently had cervical cancer, or had strong views about women's health. Individual interviews were again conducted with simple guidelines for discussion, to maximize women's opportunities to give their own accounts of services and perceptions of the personal and community contexts in which these were provided. Clinical data and observations of screening sessions and follow-up procedures provided supplementary data on the context in which women's reproductive health needs were being met.

Data Analysis

Field notes were recorded, and focus group discussions and taped interviews were transcribed and entered into a computer regularly, by two of the non-Indigenous researchers, to enable iteration. Data were analyzed thematically with word processing search functions rather than a qualitative data manager, with codes evolving as data were collected. Individual narratives of cervical cancer diagnosis and treatment were analyzed chronologically to tease out delays in treatment and care (Miles and Huberman, 1994; Weitzman and Miles, 1995; Ezzy, 2002).

RESULTS

The Ethics of Collaboration

The conduct of the research was influenced by the relationships among and shared objectives of the researchers, and between the researchers and community women. Historically much research has been conducted with Indigenous Australians without consultation or involvement. Even when protocols follow ethical guidelines designed to ensure appropriate procedures (Australia, National Health and Medical Research Council [NHMRC], 1991; Aboriginal Coordinating Council, 1995), still researchers have fallen short of Indigenous requirements and expectations of culturally sensitive processes. The usual flow of initiative, knowledge, power and methods is from a non-Indigenous perspective; Indigenous communities are positioned as subjects (if not objects). In our case, the relationship between white researchers and the Indigenous woman who initiated the project was pre-existent and unrelated to the project. The research, as noted, was proposed by Kirk, and the researchers worked as a team to conceptualize it, develop appropriate methods and identify community members for the state reference and local liaison groups. With them, we refined the methodology and time frame, and chose the study areas.

The state reference group members were concerned that the study explored women's health from an Indigenous paradigm. Our commitment to representation and diversity among the study communities ensured wide coverage and extended stays, travelling widely to meet our commitment to community women. While collecting data, we worked closely as a team. We shared frugal living quarters with each other and with community members, participated in story telling and shared experiences with them, with attention paid to the value of learning from each other as women from different cultural backgrounds and in doing so, discovering commonalities. Emphasis was placed on transparency and shared objectives. Community negotiations, data collection and analysis were all undertaken either by the Indigenous researcher alone or in partnership with the non-Indigenous researchers. This meant an inversion of the usual research paradigm and mode of operation in Australia.

Kirk was persistent that we understood each other's motivations in working in Indigenous Australia, and transferred her understandings of our standpoints to other women. This was important in terms of their acceptance of us and their willingness to be involved. Kirk was answerable to these women who were–for good historical reasons–suspicious of any researcher (Indigenous or not). She placed considerable importance also on our intent to ensure practical outcomes of the study. Her responsibility to study participants was imparted to us in ways that ensured a two-way flow of knowledge and action for the duration of and subsequent to the research. There were also inevitable exchanges of ideas and informal discussions about contemporary health problems affecting Indigenous Australians unrelated to cervical cancer, such as young people's health, other personal and family health problems, and matters related to the diagnosis, treatment and care of women with other types of cancer, including mammography screening and breast disease. These latter concerns led to a second research project on screening, diagnosis, treatment and palliative care for breast cancer (McMichael et al., 2000).

The research team frequently met with women who had been told they had an abnormal Pap smear but had not been followed up, nor had they sought follow-up advice themselves for fear of being told they have cancer or a sexually transmitted infection, as occurred in remote north Queensland:

> A woman had a Pap smear attended in September 1996, which was abnormal, and 12 months later she had not been followed-up. No health practitioner had sent her a letter or visited her, despite the existence of a follow-up and recall system in the community. When we met her, we were able to counsel her and she is now being treated. (Kirk et al., 1998b)

Findings drew attention to issues that influenced women's first and subsequent attendance for screening. Gender of provider, confusion between Pap smears and STD tests, perception of being "too young" or "too old" to be at risk of cancer or to have a test, shame, embarrassment of the procedure, and fear of a cancer diagnosis all discouraged presentation. Women were discouraged from presenting by their lack of understanding of the advantages of screening, confusion regarding appointment procedures, lack of flexibility of appointment times to allow women to present at a time other than that set for them, and distrust of health facilities and staff. These factors were compounded by contextual issues including indirect costs, lack of access to local transport, and alienation from mobile or fixed delivery mainstream services (Kirk et al., 1998a).

Indigenous Understandings of Health

Among Indigenous Australians, concepts of health embrace a complex web of relationships involving the land and the social, physical, emotional and spiritual being of people and their communities (Reid and Trompf, 1991; Hunter, 1993). Women often drew on these concepts, although their views were not homogenous. Each person's understanding is influenced by his or her own personal experiences and wider social, cultural and structural factors. Women related health to spirituality, connections with the land, and how individuals related to each other: "Health is very holistic, your identity, where you belong, where you belong in the community, where your country is. That is what health is for us" (urban woman). At the same time, concepts of health were influenced by exposure to different medical and cultural systems, and women with the least involvement in traditional cultural settings (i.e., urban women) were more likely to think of health in physical and biological terms: "In some places Aboriginal people are still hooked to the land, but a lot of people are like me who are naïve about those things. Not everyone thinks in Aboriginal ways . . . I think the upcoming women don't really care about women's business" (remote woman).

Significantly, women emphasized family and community in defining health, and not–as is common in the literature on Indigenous concepts of health and illness–the relationship to land, or the nexus of body, land and spirit (Reid, 1982; Willis, 1999; Ishtar, 2005a). The healthy body was rarely conceived of in a biological framework, but at the centre of social relationships (see Chrisman et al., 1999 for comparable data for Yakama women). Many women felt that it was important to have good health for the sake of the family, and saw good health as a state that reflected good relations within a family. Women conceived of health not just as the absence of disease, but in relation to their ability to perform daily activities and fulfil family roles; they commented that when a woman is healthy, she feels good and is capable of doing things.

While women were concerned to maintain good health, behavioral change in relation to positive health took lower precedence in daily life. Rather than taking measures to prevent illness, women tended to respond when symptoms of an illness physically manifested. Women were generally reluctant to present for follow-up or to spend an extended time away from their community for treatment: they emphasized their responsibility to others over their own health needs. In addition, women's willingness to present for care was influenced by the presence or absence of cultural safety. Cultural safety in Australia, as for Maori in New Zealand, implies central acknowledgement of the validity of cultural values (Ramsden, 1990; Smith, 1999). This was frequently expressed in relation to the social and geographic environment, including where medical examinations were conducted and whether privacy and confidentiality were assured, and in association with the timing and location of screening, interactions with health providers, and the mechanisms of reporting and follow-up.

Recommendations for Change

Feedback to communities was provided through our regular communication with the state-wide reference and local liaison groups, and through dissemination strategies including the distribution of community reports to community members in face-to-face meetings. The community reports and the full report and executive summary to Queensland Health included extensive use of quotes, vignettes, photographs and case studies, reflecting the insistence of Kirk and the women on the state reference group that women's voices be heard. This meant that the reporting style and content were distinctive from other government documents, reassuring the Indigenous women who participated in the study that they had been treated seriously. The reports provided the women who participated, and others, with a vehicle for their advocacy. Follow-up activities to the cervical cancer project, which involved the dissemination of our findings to the communities, allowed us to canvass their views about the value of a subsequent study on breast cancer.

In our recommendations, we emphasized the need for a women's health program to be developed in partnership with local women, based on an Indigenous community development model (Phillips, 2003; Ishtar, 2005a, 2005b). Services should be accessible and appropriate for Indigenous women, based on their identified local health needs. For this to work, a competency-based, accredited Women's Health Training Program was needed for all women's health practitioners, i.e., Aboriginal Health Workers, registered nurses and medical practitioners in Queensland. At the same time, in response to the particular needs of Indigenous women with cancer, a strategy was needed to establish an Indigenous Cancer Support Service in Brisbane and regional centres, with provision for community networks. We emphasized the need for a central Pap smear registry and its ongoing maintenance, and training programs, in-service education packages and support services to women's health practitioners in establishing, using and maintaining locally appropriate, "user friendly" Pap smear follow-up and recall systems.

Women's perception of existing medical services as unsympathetic pointed to the need for cross-cultural awareness, education and training for all Queensland Health Services. We argued that Queensland Health Indigenous Health Programs should take the responsibility for and provide guidance to develop a broad range of health promotional strategies at community and state levels, with community women providing input into health promotional strategies and participating as key health promoters. This program would support community women's efforts to develop and disseminate locally appropriate and culturally safe health promotion materials and resources, including for cervical cancer prevention, and would be responsible for distributing, monitoring and evaluating the materials. Communication, including Pap smear reminder messages, should use appropriate Indigenous cultural messages, language and media such as poems and stories. We also recommended that, in collaboration with community members and health practitioners, a code of best practice be developed to maintain a high quality of care and to ensure that all women receive medical attention, support, understanding and treatment regardless of their economic status, linguistic skills, race or community identity.

Outcomes

The conclusion of the study on cervical cancer was only the beginning of the process: it provided the evidence for and momentum to revise the state strategy for cervical cancer screening and to develop interventions for Indigenous health workers. Kirk was appointed as a Project Officer within the Women's Cancer Screening Unit in October 1997. She ceased her involvement as an active researcher at this stage, and instead commenced work on the public release of the report and the dissemination of findings. At the final meeting of the state reference group (5 November 1997), the group agreed to continue to support Kirk in this new capacity (Kirk et al., 1998a: Appendices, p. 7). Through the first half of 1998, with additional funds from the Women's Cancer Screening Unit and in collaboration with its staff, Kirk, the research team and members of the state reference group planned the formal launch and a workshop for Indigenous health workers, including those who had belonged to local liaison groups. The launch that preceded the workshop was held outdoors; it opened with a traditional Welcome to Land by a tribal elder, followed by various speeches, Indigenous dance performances and refreshments. The Director General of Health, in his speech, spoke of the study as "landmark" research on Indigenous health in Australia. The launch provided powerful public acknowledgement at the highest political levels of the impact of cervical cancer on Indigenous women's health and of the social and structural barriers that impact on timely and effective screening. It also provided an opportunity for Indigenous Australians to celebrate their own culture and to take ownership of the report and its recommendations.

Held in June 1998, the workshop drew on the approach adopted in *Health Workers for Change* (WHO/TDR 1997; see also Fonn and Xaba,

2001) and involved Indigenous and non-Indigenous women in ways that were powerful and confrontational. Women gave testimony to their decisions to become health workers, often following life experiences that, while no different from the stories of many Indigenous Australians (Hunter, 1993), were harrowing to witness (Manderson et al., 2001). The workshop consolidated the commitment of government officers responsible for, or part of the Women's Cancer Screening Unit, to make changes in policies and programs; enabled community health workers to meet with Queensland Health officers and helped them to gain confidence in the sincerity of the officers to act on the study recommendations; strengthened community solidarity among health workers and department officers in ways that would ensure continued communication and support; and identified mechanisms for support. The workshop concluded with a smoking ceremony, a powerful symbol of Indigenous healing. From this time, the community retained ownership of the report, the actions to follow from it, and mechanisms to support local health workers that were developed in the workshop.

The strategic plan (Queensland Health, 2000), based on the report recommendations, was developed within the Women's Cancer Screening Unit by Kirk and other government officers, again with advice from the state reference group. Concurrently (1999-2000), money was committed for further research, using the same model of advocacy and participatory research, on women's access to and use of mammography services, breast cancer diagnosis and treatment, and palliative care (Kirk et al., 2000; McMichael et al., 2000). Strategic planning, policy development and programs within the Women's Cancer Screening Unit proceeded, with the Director of the Unit now negotiating with her supervisors to ensure that Indigenous women's health remained on the agenda, that it be treated seriously as a "public health problem" and that the recommendations were enacted. In 2000, Kirk received a Queensland Health Award for Outstanding Achievement for her work with Indigenous women, particularly her research, policy, and program development activities and her personal commitment to the improvement of Indigenous women's health. While her personal commitment was a powerful factor in propelling change, and her death (in 2001) had the potential to reduce the impetus of knowledge transfer, implementation and action, political will to change within the government had been established and work continued to ensure institutional and structural changes.

The outcome was the development of the *Queensland Indigenous Women's Cervical Screening Strategy 2000-2004* (Queensland Health,

2000) and the Queensland Cervical Screening Program Phase 3 State Plan 2002-2006 (Queensland Health, 2002), which acknowledged "cultural safety" as a key component of services to improve the health of Indigenous women. Its public launch again occurred with substantial Indigenous input. As a direct consequence, Indigenous nurse practitioners were trained to work with mobile health services, mobile women's health services introduced both breast and cervical screening with other health services, and greater numbers of local Indigenous health workers were involved in these services. A zonal network of Indigenous women health workers was established to address problems of isolation and overload, and lack of regular supervision and debriefing, which, as identified in research interviews, and at the workshop, contributed substantially to burnout.[1] Cancer support systems were developed, with the local liaison women who contributed to our study becoming part of this network. At time of writing, this is under evaluation.

The research reports and subsequent policy documents provided leverage and guidelines for action, and as illustrated above, major changes to services ensued. It is too early to establish whether cancer outcomes have improved or if fewer deaths have resulted from preventive screening, but a substantial cultural shift is evident within government and its services to meet the needs of Indigenous women. Australian and state governments are still struggling with how to introduce culturally appropriate services in ways that go beyond cultural awareness training for non-Indigenous staff. However, notable changes have occurred within Queensland Health at policy and program levels, from the most senior levels of government to zonal networks of health workers working with community women, not only in cancer screening services but also in the provision of personal support for women receiving treatment, and for loss and grief counselling.

DISCUSSION

Growing attention has been given to the need for and importance of partnerships in research and practice: shared objectives, transparency, purpose and outcomes (Smith, 2002). For example, Henderson et al. (2002) have described the Koorie Health Partnership Committee, established in 1999 to develop specific research projects and review the activities of the Department (now School) of Rural Health of The University of Melbourne. The Committee's role has been to ensure a sustained partnership between academic researchers and Indigenous communities (known locally as Koorie) in northeast Victoria and southern New South Wales, Australia. The procedures for research, in place under the guidelines developed by the committee, are informed by a culturally sensitive approach and designed to ensure outcome-based policies, and by the mechanisms of consultation and involvement which transcend the conventional protocol for collaboration between academics and Indigenous people. This approach, and those of other researchers (e.g., Ishtar, 2005a, 2005b), is similar to that which we adopted.

We established a way of working with Indigenous women on health issues that acknowledged the need for action to follow from research (i.e., tangible outcomes), with community credibility and commitment to technical expertise to ensure the translation of research findings into policies and programs (i.e., impact). The power to effect change–in this example, major changes in the delivery of cervical cancer screening and treatment, and subsequently in mammography and treatment for breast cancer–derived not from the judicious mix of individuals (Indigenous and other, from government, community and academic backgrounds, of various professional and personal backgrounds), but as a result of their constituencies. The support and involvement of both community women and officers of the relevant agency, and their co-ownership of the research, were critical to the steps that followed.

As indicated, the work in its entirety had many of the key elements of advocacy, including developing 'real' partnerships between community women and government to bring about changes in health policy and programs. The partnerships, built on transparency, shared objectives and mutual obligations and sustained by constant communication, involved female Indigenous leaders, community women, authorities within Queensland Health Women's Cancer Screening Services, and academics. These are key elements of community-based research (Phillips, 2003; Ishtar, 2005a, 2005b). As researchers such as Singer and colleagues (2005) have illustrated, community-based research participatory research processes with marginalized populations can bring about structural, policy and programmatic changes. In this study, the researchers joined with Indigenous women from rural, remote and urban Queensland communities, and with leaders in government agencies, to conduct rigorous social research that would bring about structural change. As we have noted, the initial funds enabled the research to proceed, not only by supporting direct research costs, but also by ensuring, through the participatory processes, that both state authorities and communities accepted the project and the research team, and enabled the research findings to be disseminated. The limitations of the work are clear within an epidemiological or similar paradigm, deriving from purposive sampling and self-selection to participate. Measured against other qualitative studies, however, this was an especially large study. Its rigor derives from the extensiveness of discussions with women, the iteration of the study design and the feedback to communities. Community acceptance of the study findings and recommendations, and the willingness of government officers to act upon them, provided us with further evidence of the veracity and robustness of the data.

Further funding and the clear support of government officers allowed the translation of results into policy, and for policy to translate into programs. The subsequent research on breast cancer screening, follow-up and treatment, and palliative care, again was followed by prompt uptake of recommendations and a growing awareness by other service providers of the need to ensure culturally appropriate health services. The brochure produced by Breastscreen Queensland, *Healthy Aboriginal women in mind, body and spirit* (2003), while it presumes literacy and access to mail services, offers evidence of a clear shift in understanding of the cultural factors affecting screening practice; the Aboriginal and Torres Strait Islander Project of the Royal Australian College of General Practitioners (2003), conducted in three states, made similar recommendations regarding culturally appropriate services, Indigenous involvement in planning, and the need for health education for Indigenous women. Most recently, Cancer Council Australia, supported by the National Aboriginal Community Controlled Health Organization, convened the first national forum to discuss cancer among Indigenous Australians and facilitated the collaboration of various stakeholders, including Indigenous health workers and cancer survivors (Lowenthal et al., 2005).

Advocacy continues to the present, and involves Women's Cancer Screening Service staff, academics and indigenous health workers at conferences, in radio and newspapers, and academic publications, and in community and other public health forums. In particular, the national Indigenous Health Promotion Network, which involves a number of women who were on the state-wide reference or a local liaison groups, has ensured that the issues remain a priority and become part of a national agenda to address inequalities in Indigenous health status. Such advocacy is continually needed, given the continued high incidence of cervical cancer among Indigenous women, and the need for changes in cervical cancer screening services nation-wide (O'Brien et al., 2000; Saunders et al., 2002; Condon et al., 2004). The changes implemented as a result of this project are only part of a broad-based program that is beginning to redress inequities in Indigenous health and wellbeing.

NOTE

1. Many of these women are responsible not only for supporting women with cancer, but also for a wide range of health problems and traumatic outcomes (domestic violence, child abuse, suicide, frequent incarceration and drug and alcohol misuse in addition to high prevalence of and early mortality from non-communicable diseases).

REFERENCES

Australia, 1989. *National Women's Health Policy*. Canberra: Australian Government Publishing Service.

Australian Bureau of Statistics, 2006. *Year Book Australia 2006. http://www.abs. gov.au/Ausstats/*, Accessed 20 January 2006.

Australia, National Health and Medical Research Council, 1991. *Guidelines on Ethical Matters in Aboriginal and Torres Strait Islander Health Research, Approved by the 111th Session of the National Health and Medical Research Council, Brisbane, June 1991*. Canberra: Australian Government Publishing Service.

Aboriginal Coordinating Council, 1995. *Consultation Protocols: How to Consult Appropriately and Effectively with Aboriginal or Torres Strait Islander Communities*. Brisbane: Queensland Health.

Austin, D. 2004. Partnerships, not projects! Improving the environment through collaborative research and action. *Human Organization* 63, 4: 419-430.

Chrisman, N.J., Strickland, J., Powell, K., Squeochs, M.D. and Yallup, M. 1999. Community partnership research with the Yakama Indian Nation. *Human Organization* 58, 2: 134-141.

Condon, J.R., Barnes, T., Cunningham, J. and Armstrong, B.K. 2004. Long-term trends in cancer mortality for Indigenous Australians in the Northern Territory. *Medical Journal of Australia* 180: 504-507.

Condon, J.R., Barnes, T., Armstrong, B.K., Selva-Nayagam, S. and Elwood, J.M. 2005. Stage at diagnosis and cancer survival for Indigenous Australians in the Northern Territory. *Medical Journal of Australia* 182: 277-280.

Coory, M.D., Thompson, A. and Ganguly, I. 2000. Cancer among people living in rural and remote Indigenous communities in Queensland. *Medical Journal of Australia* 173: 301-304.

Coory, M.D., Fagan, P.S., Muller, J.M. and Dunn, N.A.M. 2002. Participation in cervical cancer screening by women in rural and remote Aboriginal and Torres Strait Islander communities in Queensland. *Medical Journal of Australia* 177: 544-547.

De Souza, R. 2004. Motherhood, migration and methodology: Giving voice to the "other." *The Qualitative Report* 9, 3: 463-482.

Ezzy, D. 2002. *Qualitative Analysis. Practice and innovation*. Sydney: Allen & Unwin.

Eades, S.J., Read, A.W. and Bibbulung Gnarneep Team, 1999. The Bibbulung Gnarneep Project: Practical implementation of guidelines on ethics in Indigenous health research. *Medical Journal of Australia* 170: 433-436.

Fonn, S, and Xaba, M. 2001. Health workers for change: Developing the initiative. *Health Policy and Planning* 16, Suppl. 1: 13-18.

Henderson, R., Simmons, D.S., Bourke, L. and Muir, J. 2002. Development of guidelines for non-Indigenous people undertaking research among the Indigenous population of north-east Victoria. *Medical Journal of Australia* 176: 462-485.

Hunter, E. 1993 *Aboriginal Heath and History.* Melbourne: Cambridge University Press.

De Ishtar, Z. 2005a. Striving for a common language: A white feminist parallel to Indegenous ways on knowing and researching. *Women's Studies International Forum* 28: 357-368.

De Ishtar, Z. 2005b. Living on the ground: The "culture woman" and the "missus." *Women's Studies International Forum* 28: 369-380.

Kirk, M. 1993. An Aboriginal perspective on cancer. *Aboriginal and Islander Health Worker Journal* 17, 3: 11-13.

Kirk, M., Carr, B., Angus, S. and Boyle, F. 1995 *Prevention and Early Detection of Cancer in Aboriginal and Torres Strait Islander Women.* Brisbane: Royal Women's Hospital.

Kirk, M., Hoban, E., Dunne, A. and Manderson, L. 1998a. *Barriers to and Appropriate Delivery Systems for Cervical Cancer Screening in Indigenous Communities in Queensland. Final Report.* Brisbane: Government Press.

Kirk, M., Hoban, E., Dunne, A. and Manderson, L. 1998b. *Barriers to and Appropriate Delivery Systems for Cervical Cancer Screening Services in Indigenous Communities in Queensland: Remote Indigenous Communities.* Report to Queensland Health, Women's Cancer Screening Services. Brisbane: Queensland Health.

Kirk, M., McMichael, C., Potts, H., Hoban, E., Hill, D.C. and Manderson, L. 2000. *Breast Cancer: Screening, Diagnosis, Treatment and Care for Aboriginal and Torres Strait Islander Women in Queensland. Final Report.* Brisbane: Queensland Health.

Lamphere, L. 2004. The convergence of applied, practicing, and public anthropology in the 21st century. *Human Organization* 63, 4: 431-443.

Lowenthal, R.M., Grogan, P.B. and Kerrins, E.T. 2005. Reducing the impact of cancer in Indigenous communities: Ways forward. *Medical Journal of Australia* 182: 105-106.

Manderson, L., Kelaher, M., Williams, G. and Shannon, C. 1998. The politics of community: Negotiation and consultation in research on women's health. *Human Organization* 57, 2: 222-239.

Manderson, L., Kirk, M. and Hoban, E. 2001. Walking the talk: Research partnerships in women's business. In I. Dyck, N. D. Lewis and S. McLafferty (Eds.), *Geographies of Women's Health.* New York and London: Routledge, pp.177-194.

McMichael, C., Kirk, M. Manderson, L., Hoban, E. and Potts, H. 2000. Indigenous women's perceptions of breast cancer diagnosis and treatment in Queensland. *Australian and New Zealand Journal of Public Health* 24(5): 515-519.

Miles, M. and Huberman, A.M. 1994 (2nd Ed). *Qualitative Data Analysis. An Expanded Sourcebook.* London: SAGE Publications

Minkler, M. and Wallerstein, N. 2003. *Community-Based Participatory Research Health.* San Francisco: Jossey-Bass.

O'Brien, E.D., Bailie, R.S. and Jelfs, P.L. 2000. Cervical cancer mortality in Australia: Contrasting risk by Aboriginality, age and rurality. *International Journal of Epidemiology* 29 (5): 813-816.

Panaretto, K.S., Larkins, S. and Manessis, V. 2003. Pap smear participation rates, primary healthcare and Indigenous women. *Medical Journal of Australia* 178: 525.
Phillips, G. 2003. *Addictions and Healing in Aboriginal Country*. Canberra: AIATSIS.
Queensland Health, 1992. *Queensland Health Indigenous Workforce Management Strategy (1992-2002)*. Brisbane: Queensland Health
Queensland Health, 1993. *Queensland Government Women's Health Policy*. Brisbane: Queensland Health.
Queensland Health, 1994. *Aboriginal and Torres Strait Islander Health Policy 1994*. Brisbane: Aboriginal and Torres Strait Islander Health Branch, Queensland Health.
Queensland Health, 1998a. *Aboriginal and Torres Strait Islander Cross-Cultural Awareness Minimum Standards*. Brisbane: Queensland Health.
Queensland Health, 1998b. *Meeting the Challenge–Better Health for Indigenous Queenslanders*. Brisbane: Queensland Health.
Queensland Health, 2000. *Queensland Indigenous Women's Cervical Screening Strategy 2000-2004*. Brisbane: Queensland Health
Queensland Health, 2002. *Queensland Cervical Screening Program Phase 3 State Plan 2002-2006*. Brisbane: Queensland Health.
Ramsden, I. 1990. *Whakaruruhau: Cultural Safety in Nursing Education in Aotearoa*. Auckland: Maori Health and Nursing, Ministry of Education, Government of New Zealand.
Reid, J.C. (ed.), 1982. *Body, Land and Spirit: Health and Healing in Aboriginal Society*. Brisbane: University of Queensland Press.
Reid, J.C. and Trompf, P. (eds.), 1991. *The Health of Aboriginal Australia*. Sydney: Harcourt, Brace, Jovanovich.
Saunders, V., Elston, J. and Gennat, H. 2002. *Early Detection and Management of Breast and Cervical Cancer in Aboriginal and Torres Strait Islander Women: Supporting the Role of the General Practitioner*. Townsville: School of Public Health and Tropical Medicine, James Cook University.
Schensul, J.J. and Stern, G. 1985. Introduction: Collaborative research and social action. *American Behavioral Scientist* 29: 133-138.
Singer, M., Stopka, T., Shaw, S., Santilices, C., Buchanan, D., Teng, W., Khoosnood, K. and Heimer, R. 2005. Lessons from the field: From research to application in the fight against AIDS among injection drug users in three New England cities. *Human Organization* 64, 2: 179-191.
Smith, L.T. 1999. *Decolonizing Methodologies*. New York: University of Otago Press
Stull, D.D. and Schensul, J.J. (eds.), 1987. *Collaborative Research and Social Change: Applied Anthropology in Action*. Boulder, Col.: Westview Press.
Weitzman, E. and Miles, M. 1995. *Computer Programs for Qualitative Data Analysis*. Thousand Oaks: SAGE Publications
WHO/TDR (United Nations Development Programme/World Bank/World Health Organization. Special Programme for Research and Training in Tropical Diseases, 1997. *Health Workers for Change. A Manual to Improve Quality of Care*. Women's Health Project, Johannesburg, South Africa.
Willis J. 1999. Dying in country: Implications of culture in the delivery of palliative care in indigenous Australian communities. *Anthropology and Medicine* 6, 3: 423-427.

doi:10.1300/J013v43n04_05

Using Participatory Research to Build an Effective Type 2 Diabetes Intervention: The Process of Advocacy Among Female Hispanic Farmworkers and Their Families in Southeast Idaho

Elizabeth Cartwright, PhD
Diana Schow, MA
Silvia Herrera
Yezenia Lora
Maricela Mendez
Deborah Mitchell, BA, BS
Elizabeth Pedroza
Leticia Pedroza
Angel Trejo

SUMMARY. The *Formando Nuestro Futuro*/Shaping our Future project (herewith, *Formando*) is a community-based participative research (CBPR) focused on type 2 diabetes. It was conceptualized and designed

Elizabeth Cartwright, Diana Schow, Silvia Herrera, Yezenia Lora, Maricela Mendez, Deborah Mitchell, Elizabeth Pedroza, Leticia Pedroza, and Angel Trejo are affiliated with Hispanic Health Projects, Department of Anthropology, Box 8005, Idaho State University, Pocatello, ID 83209.

[Haworth co-indexing entry note]: "Using Participatory Research to Build an Effective Type 2 Diabetes Intervention: The Process of Advocacy Among Female Hispanic Farmworkers and Their Families in Southeast Idaho." Cartwright, Elizabeth et al. Co-published simultaneously in *Women & Health* (The Haworth Medical Press, an imprint of The Haworth Press, Inc.) Vol. 43, No. 4, 2006, pp. 89-109; and: *Women's Health: New Frontiers in Advocacy & Social Justice Research* (ed: Elizabeth Cartwright, and Pascale Allotey) The Haworth Medical Press, an imprint of The Haworth Press, Inc., 2006, pp. 89-109. Single or multiple copies of this article are available for a fee from The Haworth Document Delivery Service [1-800-HAWORTH, 9:00 a.m. - 5:00 p.m. (EST). E-mail address: docdelivery@haworthpress.com].

by a team of university-based researchers and community health workers (promotores). This article describes the process of establishing a CBPR project such as *Formando* and the most current results from that project. The Formando project is an example of health-focused advocacy with the Mexican agricultural workers in Southeast (SE) Idaho. To date, 172 qualitative interviews on participants' knowledge about type 2 diabetes have been carried out with farmworker women and their families. Biometric data (heights, weights, blood pressures and fasting blood glucoses) were obtained from participants. Fieldnotes, focus group discussions and key informants were used to triangulate findings. Significant quantitative findings include that age was significantly associated with Body Mass Index (BMI) ($p < 0.001$, Spearman Correlation < 0.001) and with elevated fasting blood glucose ($p < 0.001$, Spearman Correlation < 0.001). The qualitative interviews were thematically analyzed. Key themes associated with type 2 diabetes in this community were the connection between thinness and vanity, dieting and starvation and the onset of diabetes as a result of, what social scientists call, structural violence within the immigrants' daily lives. We conclude that long-term commitment to using the CBPR approach in these Mexican agricultural communities is an effective way to engage in health research and to establish real and meaningful dialogue with community members. doi:10.1300/J013v43n04_06 *[Article copies available for a fee from The Haworth Document Delivery Service: 1-800-HAWORTH. E-mail address: <docdelivery@haworthpress.com> Website: <http://www.HaworthPress.com>* © *2006 by The Haworth Press, Inc. All rights reserved.]*

KEYWORDS. Community-based participatory research (CBPR), advocacy, Hispanic farmworkers, type 2 diabetes, community health workers (CHWs)

INTRODUCTION

Human rights violations are not accidents; they are not random in distribution or effect. Rights violations are, rather, symptoms of deeper pathologies of power and are linked intimately to the social conditions that so often determine who will suffer abuse and who will be shielded from harm. (Farmer 2003, p. 7)

In this article we first describe the long-term process of establishing our community-based health research projects with the Mexican agricultural worker[1] communties in Southeast (SE) Idaho. The research and advocacy work was done through the Hispanic Health Projects[2] (HHP)–a group of individuals dedicated to improving the health of Hispanic agricultural workers through promoting social justice at the individual, community and national levels. We then describe, in detail, the results from our first year of an on-going research and intervention program focused on type 2 diabetes.

Working from the notion that health is a human right, the HHP's research projects attend to issues of documenting and assessing Hispanic farmworker families' access to appropriate treatments and to preventive health care. The HHP team also engages in research that precisely describes individual understandings of diseases and their treatments as well as gathering biometric data that describe the burden of the disease on this particular community. Subsequently, the knowledge generated through the research projects is used to create consciousness raising and dialogue about health and social issues that are most important to the community members

The HHP is conceptualized as a three-pronged approach to understanding and changing the health of the underserved, Hispanic farmworker communities in the U.S. through research[3] (that identifies and explores health problems and raises consciousness of the issues within the community), education (of community members and the larger society), and interventions (based on the results of the research projects). Recognition of the large amount of time that it actually takes to facilitate a change in the health status of a group of individuals within a community is essential in work such as this. The HHP research and intervention programs are set up to keep working toward collective health goals until they are reached, however long that takes, and whether the goal is decreasing the prevalence of type 2 diabetes, or the rates of untreated cervical cancer, HIV/AIDS transmission, the number of pesticide poisonings, or domestic violence incidents. Real change takes time.

Oftentimes, researchers who work on health issues with Mexican agricultural workers avoid discussing and researching the parts of the bi-national realities of Mexican immigrants that relate to the contemporary immigrant experience for Mexicans who come to the U.S. to work in agriculture and other entry-level jobs. Instead, research projects focus on particular "health" problems, such as a particular disease, without contextualizing the experience of that disease within the context of what it is like to live in the U.S. as recent, often undocumented, immigrants. The realities of immigration are embedded within commonly used clinical and research vocabulary such as limited access to care, stages of acculturation, and women who arrive at the clinic for late prenatal care. Late prenatal care is as much about not getting in for a sonogram and a supply of prenatal vitamins as it is about the terror of being discovered as "illegal" when applying for services at the clinic and subsequently being deported for immigration violations. It is also about the realities of navigating the U.S. legal system, the endless hours of work needed to amass the money to make another crossing attempt of the U.S./Mexico Border, the corrupt officials in both countries and the physical and psychological dangers of crossing through that ever-more-militarized zone that divides the United States and Mexico (Heyman 1995).

The HHP's research is aimed at understanding how illnesses are experienced within particular social and cultural contexts. While many cultural differences exist in how illnesses are discussed and in what home treatments are used, the social and political realities of the immigrant situation often take precedence in both individual conceptualizations of why health problems occur as well as in, ultimately, if an individual receives treatment. The difficulties and indignities present in living as a recent immigrant in the U.S. consistently appeared in thematic analyses in our health research projects and ultimately, served as highly generative themes of discussion that facilitated a translation of our research into community action targeted at ameliorating such things as access to health care, medical interpreters and other needed resources.

Women in these farmworker families are the primary care givers within the family unit. They make the decisions about preventive strategies, family nutrition, home-based/traditional treatments for illnesses, as well as about when to use biomedical care and how and if to follow the subsequent biomedical treatment regimen. For example, in the realities of living with type 2 diabetes, the women are pivotal both in caring for their own diabetes problems, as well as for those of their spouses, older relatives and more and more often, their children. While the HHP's approach is always family-based, it is the women who are the main focus of our research and education programs.

This paper highlights the process of engaging in long-term, sustainable health research with Hispanic farmworker women and their families. We first briefly describe three research projects that have been undertaken, one after another, during the last seven years at the HHP that were designed to research health care issues and needs of the Hispanic women and their families. The inter-personal work of gaining access to families and in establishing a trustful working relationship with them is an integral part of CBPR (Brown & Vega 1996). Each research project and health education intervention is seen as another step in the process of establishing a fruitful working relationship between the academics and community members of the HHP, the Hispanic farmworker families in the region and the local health care professionals. We conclude with a discussion of insights from the *Formando* Project in the context of this process and how they can further refine our understanding of the cultural and social particulars inherent in implementing CBPR projects that are intended to raise the level of awareness about a health problem and to begin the process of helping individuals to lead healthier lives.

BACKGROUND

Hispanic Farmworkers in the United States: Hidden Populations, Hidden Health Problems. Immigration and health are inextricably intertwined in individuals coming from Mexico to work in the U.S. Until the 1930s, the U.S. did not have an immigration policy with respect to Mexico. The Bracero Accord was initiated in 1942, and during the twenty-two years of its existence this program allowed over 4.6 million temporary workers to enter the U.S. (Durand, Massey & Parrado 1999, p. 519). Between the end of the Bracero Accord in 1964 and the Reagan administration's Immigration Reform and Control Act (IRCA) of 1986, millions of documented and undocumented workers moved between the U.S. and Mexico.

The IRCA of 1986 contained new funding for two different components of immigration control. On the one hand, it included funding to hire more Border Patrol agents and increase Border infrastructure as well as increasing sanctions for U.S. employers who hired undocumented workers. Interestingly, the same bill also contained the amnesty/legalization programs the Legally Authorized Worker Program and the Special Agricultural Worker Program (Durand, Massey & Parrado 1999, p. 521). One of the goals of the IRCA was to generate a "clean slate" by legalizing those undocumented workers who could prove they had continuously been in the U.S. living and working since before January 1, 1982 (Public Law 99-603). Approximately, 2.3 million workers took advantage of these legalization programs and became permanent residents of the U.S.

In many cases, those who qualified were men who then sent for their wives and children back in Mexico to come join them in the U.S. Women and children subsequently arrived, many without legal immigration status. The net result was a vast increase in undocumented Mexicans coming to live permanently in the U.S. (Durand, Massey & Parrado 1999, p. 525). Since the IRCA was passed in 1986, these new immigrant families have tended to move into rural areas, such as SE Idaho where the HHP is located (Durand, Massey & Parrado 1999, p. 530). While the HHP never asks individuals for their immigration status, proxy data on payment methods at clinics show that over 50% of the Hispanic farmworkers in the area are probably undocumented.

According to the 2000 U.S. Census, the population of the state of Idaho is 1,293,953, of which 101,690 individuals self-identify as Hispanic or Latino (7.9%; U.S. Census Bureau Statistics 2000). In the southern half of Idaho, where the majority of Idaho's agriculture takes place, Hispanics are a much larger percentage of the overall population. This is the case in the two study sites of American Falls and Aberdeen. In the last ten years, the percentage of Hispanics in these two small Idaho towns has nearly doubled to between 30-40%. Hispanics are playing an increasingly vital role in the social and cultural life in Idaho's small, strongly religious, and conservative farming communities.

Hispanic farmworkers in the U.S. are at risk for many conditions of ill health. According to Villarejo and Baron (1999) these conditions can include poor nutrition, anemia, tuberculosis, parasitic infections, communicable diseases, diabetes, cancer, hypertension, high-risk pregnancy, respiratory problems resulting from exposure to dust, fungus, and pesticides, dehydration, heat stroke, urinary tract infections, and depression. Farmworkers in SE Idaho also experience these problems. According to the HHP's 1998-1999 community needs assessment, Hispanic agricultural workers in SE Idaho have an average annual family income of $10,000 and an average family size of five individuals, 75% have no insurance, and over 88% speak only or mostly Spanish (Hunter, Hall, Hearn, & Cartwright 2003; Early 2001; Guzzle 2000).

The Process of Community-Based Diabetes Research with Hispanic Farmworkers in SE Idaho. The HHPs have evolved over the last seven years through a process of completing several CBPR projects and health education interventions. First, a community health needs assessment survey was performed in 1998-1999. The goal of the survey was to detail overall health concerns in a general manner. The survey, based on Slesinger's (1992) similar work in the Midwest, was administered to 179 adult, Hispanic farmworkers who were currently working in either the fields or the potato processing plants. The participants were chosen from a convenience sample with a participation rate of greater than 99%. The research assistants who implemented the survey had worked or were currently doing farm labor in the study communities. The team was also composed of some bi-lingual university students. The interviewers were all trained in survey research (see Hunter, Hall, Hearn, & Cartwright 2003 for a full description of the quantitative analysis of the survey).

To clarify some of the quantitative survey results, three members of the HHP engaged in a series of in-depth qualitative interviews with forty Spanish-speaking adults (Early 2001; Guzzle 2000). The interviewees often made comparisons between the medical care in the U.S. and Mexico that allowed the research team to understand the context within which the farmworkers were judging the care that they received in Idaho. One of the interviewees made the following observation:

> In Mexico if a person cannot pay, they don't receive treatment, the doctors just tell them, "There's nothing we can do." And like my brother-in-law, he cut his hand off (doing agricultural work in Idaho). Here, in the U.S., they re-attached it. It didn't matter if he could pay or not. If that would have happened in Mexico, if you can't pay for the operation, you cut your hand off and that's it. So, (in Mexico) you don't have to pay the hospital bill, but you don't have your hand. Now I understand why we came here. (Guzzle 2000, p. 92)

In the case of life-threatening, emergency situations, farmworkers in SE Idaho do have access to care far beyond what many could expect in rural Mexico. Paying the astronomical hospital bills, after the fact, is a constant source of stress for the majority of the farmworker families in our study—but most are glad to have received the emergency medical care.

The perception of discrimination against Mexicans, both those recently immigrated as well as those born in the U.S., is an over-riding theme that has emerged regardless of the health topic under discussion. Disenfranchisement with respect to the larger, Anglo society is reinforced through serious language barriers as well as through fear and misunderstandings that abound in the small, rural, agricultural communities of SE Idaho. Basic issues of miscommunication and misunderstanding need to be considered when interpreting both survey and interview data.

Diabetes research provides a clear example of how long it takes individuals to open up about their feelings and perceptions about a serious disease. The 1998-1999 community needs assessment survey showed that diabetes was listed as a problem for only about 5% of the survey respondents and their families. This number seemed very low to those members of the research team who had experience working with this community. The reasons for this kind of under-reporting were not obvious until we had learned how to communicate more effectively about this health issue. The team agreed that surveys were of limited value in this Spanish-speaking community where immigration-related problems abound, and distrust of outsiders is quite pronounced. Following-up on the issue of diabetes, researchers at HHP engaged in clinical chart reviews of 100% of the diabetic patients seen at the local community health centers (Hunter, Cartwright, & Hall 2001). These chart reviews showed that individuals were not being diagnosed with type 2 diabetes until they were well into middle age. Also, the chart reviews demonstrated that less than 5% of the individuals at the clinic for diabetes treatment were maintaining their Hemoglobin A1c (HgA1c) and blood glucose levels according to the American Diabetes Association criteria for glycemic control. The community needs assessment combined with the chart review provided a better understanding of the health problems of the Hispanic farmworkers. Many of the findings from the initial studies were clarified and refined in the subsequent Binational Study.

In 2001, the HHP engaged in a binational ethnographic project that was designed to describe how Hispanic farmworker families treat acute and chronic illnesses. It was during this research project that we began to understand the true magnitude of the problems associated with diabetes in these communities (Cartwright & Schaper 2002). A team of university researchers, promotores (community health workers) and students went to Dolores Hidalgo, Guanajuato, Mexico, at the invitation of some of the Mexican promotores who were among the first HHP research assistants. The close working conditions and the inter-dependence between the academics and promotores resulted in personal relationships that were based on a real understanding of each other and their importance cannot be overstated.

During the binational ethnographic project, individual treatment-seeking behaviors were described within the context of how families develop strategies to allocate their local and binational resources to obtain treatments and medications. Qualitative interviews describing treatment strategies were carried out with a convenience sample of 150 Hispanic families who were currently employed in agricultural work or in the potato processing plants (100 in SE Idaho and 50 in the sending communities in Guanajuato, Mexico). Participation rates were better than 95%. These interviews focused on how adults and children in the households used traditional, in-home treatments, local healing experts (*curanderos*, *parteras*, and *sobadoras*), medical doctors, and pharmaceuticals for specific illnesses. Current physical status of household members was assessed using basic biomedical tests to screen for diabetes (elevated blood sugars), hypertension and weight problems. Individual's personal understandings or models of diabetes and cancer were also elaborated during the interviews, and, when appropriate, explanatory models were explored for other illness categories that were especially important to a particular individual.

To describe the problem of type 2 diabetes in this population, a significant portion of the qualitative interviews were dedicated to a careful exploration of people's ideas about where diabetes comes from, how it affects them, personal experiences with diabetes in their families, and what it means for individuals in these two communities to have diabetes. Individuals described to us how diabetes came from such things as *herencia* (heredity), *mala nutrición* (poor nutrition), and *gordura* (obesity). These are among the causes recognized by medical doctors and described in other studies (Weller et al. 1999). Individuals in the binational study attributed their diabetes to such ultimate causes as *susto* (fright), *coraje* (anger), and *preocupaciónes* (worries). Thematic analysis of *susto, coraje* and *nervios* show that these emotions were used to index both a sense of personal stress about individual problems (domestic violence, accidents, etc.) as well as the larger stresses that are so pervasive among these families including having family members *"al otro lado"* (out of the country), fears of deportation, violence experienced in border crossings and discrimination.

Thematic analysis of the interviews also demonstrated that ideas about diabetes were linked with ideas of personal susceptibility; having diabetes was a stigmatized condition that connoted weakness. Individuals who were diabetic were seen as vulnerable to being shocked and physically harmed by situations that others could withstand. For instance, a study participant described how bad news was kept from a diabetic grandfather for fear of shocking him—the shock could have resulted in his collapsing or dying. Individuals with diabetes were seen as weaker than other people (see also Ferzacca 2000).

One of the tenets of CBPR is that the community has control over the process of identifying health problems; yet sometimes community members do not have adequate information to make informed decisions. In the communities where we worked, it was not uncommon to encounter individuals who did not know whether they had elevated blood glucose levels or increased blood pressure. They also did not understand the health ramifications of having either of these conditions. Once biometric data was provided to them in a non-threatening and easy to understand manner, they became much more interested in learning about diabetes. This binational study provided us with data from one point in time and with a good working knowledge of some of the cultural and social issues surrounding diabetes that needed to be explored in more depth and across time.

FORMANDO NUESTRO FUTURO: *A FIVE-YEAR COMMUNITY-BASED DIABETES RESEARCH PROJECT*

Study Design

> In problem-posing education, people develop their power to perceive critically the way they exist in the world with which and in which they find themselves; they come to see the world not as a static reality, but as a reality in process, in transformation. (Freire 1970, p. 83)

The current diabetes project, *Formando*, has been underway since May 2004. The process of conceptualizing the project as well as the study design, methods, findings and discussion of the first year's results will be included here. The *Formando* project is an example of individual and family level advocacy and research. *Formando* was based on the Freirian concept of dialogic education and community consciousness-raising.

The *Formando* project is being carried out from 2004 to 2009 in the small, agricultural communities of American Falls and Aberdeen, Idaho. A target of 250 individuals aged twelve years and up (out of a total of 1,600 adult individuals who self-identified as "Hispanic" on the 2000 Census) will be enrolled from the Hispanic farmworkers who live (either year-round, or seasonally) in these communities. To be included in the Formando project, at least one individual in the family must be working or have worked in agriculture at some time. Inclusion was broadened to include adolescents and retired adults from the more strict inclusion criteria in our previous studies. This was to provide for a full description of the disease process of type 2 diabetes. Participation rates have been better than 95%, with less than 10 individuals refusing participation.

Individuals are being recruited from several different sources. First, because the HHP has been working in the area for several years, many women and their families are personally known by the promotores. All families whom have had contact with HHP in the past for the Saturday Women's clinics, Salsa Aerobics and research projects and who still are living in the area have been invited to participate in the *Formando* diabetes project. Participation in the healthy cooking and aerobics classes will be taken into account in the final statistical analyses. Participants gave us the names of other families to contact with invitations to participate. This snowball method of recruitment (Rice & Ezzy 1999) has worked well in the past. To recruit from the community at large and avoid selection bias, announcements were made in Spanish and English on radio programs and in local newspapers. Informational flyers about the diabetes project were also posted at local stores, churches, laundromats and restaurants. Local health care providers have also begun to refer individuals and their families who would, for whatever reason, be interested in learning more about diabetes and general health issues. These multiple types of study recruitment are appropriate given the lack of census or other list of Hispanic farmworkers and also recognizing that about ten percent of the farmworkers in this area move frequently (Hunter, Hall, Hearn & Cartwright 2003), thus the need for radio, Spanish language newspapers and flyers at local businesses to make sure that the more mobile part of the population is represented to the fullest extent possible.

Data Collection

The *Formando* study uses quantitative and qualitative methods to document patterns of elevated blood glucose levels, BMIs, and blood pressure often associated with insulin resistance and type 2 diabetes. The data gathering, interviewing and attendant education components are being implemented by the promotores and are designed to encourage community participation in the research project through increasing understanding of the disease process and the ways in which individuals can prevent type 2 diabetes and/or care for family members who have the disease. Participants' questions are answered verbally during the home visit and form the basis of subsequent research topics; the questions are analyzed by the HHP team and form the basis of subsequent educational materials. In Year One, the answers were written down by the promotores; in subsequent years the answers will be tape-recorded and transcribed in their entirety. The particular difficulties of living with diabetes are discussed during the home visits. Additionally, the social themes of the stigma of being diagnosed with diabetes and the lack of access to clinical care are also addressed by the promotores. It is through attending to these more social themes, in Freire's (1970) terms, generative themes, that individuals can also become engaged in changing unhealthy aspects of their lifestyles.

> To investigate the generative theme is to investigate people's thinking about reality and people's action upon reality, which is their praxis. For precisely this reason, the methodology proposed requires that the investigators and the people (who would normally be considered objects of that investigation) should act as co-investigators. (Freire 1970, p. 106)

METHODS

Formando was conceptualized with the idea of sharing the findings with the participants as the study progressed, as well as through addressing participants' questions during the process. Each study family is visited by the promtores once or twice during the year.[4] At each home visit, all family members age twelve years and up who wish to participate are provided with their fasting blood glucose levels as well as with their blood pressure, heights, weights and their body mass indices (BMIs). The results of the monitoring values are discussed with the individuals at the time of the visit, and the participants are given their results in writing and are encouraged to take them along to the clinic when they have their next appointment. Any individuals who have abnormal blood glucose or blood pressure readings are double-checked the following day and then counseled to go into the community health clinic if the readings remain above normal. As part of their work at the HHP, the promotores facilitate setting up the clinic appointments for the study participants and will provide interpreting at the medical appointments, if it is needed.

A series of education modules are being presented at each home visit throughout the five-year study. These education modules are based on the questions that the participants had during the previous round of visits from the promotores. Using local illness terms and addressing local ideas pertaining to type 2 diabetes is an important part of creating effective education programs (Brown et al. 2002; Fisher et al. 2002). During each round of visits, different aspects of local perceptions of diabetes are documented through short answer questionnaires as well as through in-depth interviews that elicit culturally specific explanatory models of how diabetes works and how individuals are treating it. All home visits and interviews are carried out by promotores (five females and one male) and, when appropriate, by university faculty and or students who are involved in the project.

The initial interviews were focused on obtaining a detailed understanding of individuals' ideas about where diabetes comes from, how you get it, the bodily symptoms associated with the illness and how it can be treated (see Stein 1985; Schoenberg, Ameyu & Coward 1998). Body image ideas and the cultural meanings of being overweight are also being explored with women and men of various ages (including adolescents) within the households. The condition of obesity has profound ramifications with respect to the abnormal metabolism of blood glucose–less well understood are the social and cultural meanings associated with being overweight during various times of the life cycle. The following section is a summation of the most seminal results from Year One of the study

FINDINGS

Quantitative Results. The basic, descriptive statistics, including percentage distributions of participants' BMIs, ages and FBGs (see Tables 1 and 2) show that the vast majority of participants were clinically overweight or obese and that weight was greater in older participants.

Fasting blood glucose levels clearly tended to increase with age. We included the category "High Normal" as an educational tool. While a fasting blood glucose between 91 and 99 mg/dl is not diagnostic for pre-diabetes, individuals with this level who are aware of the relationship between abnormally high FBG and weight gain may be motivated

TABLE 1. Body Mass Index (BMI) by Age Categories

BMI	< 21 years	21-39 years	40-49 years	> 50 years	Total
Normal (< 24.9)	63.9% (23)	16.4% (11)	16.6% (6)	3.0% (1)	23.8% (41)
Overweight (25-29.9)	19.4% (7)	43.3% (29)	27.8% (10)	48.5% (16)	36.0% (62)
Obese (>=30)	16.7% (6)	40.3% (27)	55.6% (20)	48.5% (16)	40.1% (69)
Percentage of total responses n = 172	100.0% (36)	100.0% (67)	100.0% (36)	100.0% (33)	100.0% (172)

$p < 0.001$, Spearman Correlation < 0.001

TABLE 2. Fasting Blood Glucose by Age

FBG mg/dl	< 21 years	21-39 years	40-49 years	> 50 years	Total
Normal (< 90)	94.1% (32)	83.8% (57)	69.4% (25)	60.6% (20)	78.4% (134)
High Normal (90-99)	5.9% (2)	10.3% (7)	16.7% (6)	9.1% (3)	10.5% (18)
Pre-Diabetes/Type 2 (100 up)	0.0% (0)	5.9% (4)	13.9% (5)	30.3% (10)	11.1% (19)
Percental of total responses n = 171	100.0% (34)	100.0% (68)	100.0% (36)	100.0% (33)	100.0% (171)

p < 0.001, Spearman Correlation < 0.001

to make behavioral changes. One of the findings from the initial discussions between the promotores and the participants about the basic type 2 diabetes, was that once diagnosed, individuals felt they could do little, and some, because of this hopelessness, did little or nothing;[5] for some, even taking their prescribed medications was seen as useless and being asked to give up one's favorite food or beverage was seen as a punitive measure much resented by both women and men.

Qualitative Results. The analysis of the interviews identified the basic themes from ten short answer interview questions in the Year One encounters. Responses were tallied and grouped together using accepted principles of thematic analysis (Ryan & Bernard 2003). Intercoder reliability was performed by having the results of the thematic analysis reviewed by all members of the HHP team. Once agreement was attained, field notes and observations were used to triangulate and explain the meanings of the themes. Year Two data will be tape-recorded narratives which should contribute even richer detail.

Participation in *Formando* is open to all community members. Two-thirds of the families in the project had at least one close family member who had been diagnosed with type 2 diabetes or with pre-diabetes in contrast to the result from the original community assessment in which only 5% of families answered that type 2 diabetes was a problem encountered in their families (Hunter, Hall, Hearn & Cartwright 2003). The *Formando* project showed that in many cases, one individual in the household will have been diagnosed with type 2 diabetes many years prior, and the other adults and adolescents in the family did not have even a basic understanding about what diabetes is, its risk factors or how it can be controlled.

Thus, as the HHP team shared the results of the blood glucose tests and discussed how increased weight and increased fasting blood glucose levels are closely related with the *Formando* participants, we examined the reaction of the women in the families–because, in most cases, it is the women who make the changes in the quality and quantity of food consumed. Their husbands, parents, in-laws and the culture itself have expectations of the Hispanic women's meal preparation, especially when the meals are part of the many celebrations held throughout the year. Not to engage in eating the *carnitas, posole, tortillas, frijoles,* and *pasteles,* is seen as not joining in, as holding oneself aloof. To be on a diet is to *"matarse de hambre"* to kill oneself from hunger. Even the term "healthy cooking," *"cocinando saludable,"* is associated with food that is overly expensive and lacks flavor and sufficient quantity to render one feeling "full" (*llenarse*). To feel full is important and seen as the marker for when one should stop eating. Until that feeling is attained, individuals believe that they can and should continue eating. In our binational study, many individuals in Mexico were subsisting on a couple of tortillas a day for weeks or months at a time when remittances from their spouses in the U.S. were slow in coming or when subsistence crops failed. As one of the promotores noted, "People believe if they have gone to all the trouble to come here to the U.S. they should be able to eat well." The experience of hunger leaves an indelible mark; recent experiences of hunger as well as childhood memories of being hungry contribute to a strong desire to eating one's fill if the food is available according to the study participants.

Ironically, several of the participants from the aerobics classes who had been successful at losing weight encountered the community opinion that by losing weight they were engaging in an act of vanity which was not consistent with having humility before God. Some of the men pressured their wives not to continue with the aerobics when they saw them losing weight and gaining in self-esteem; conversely, some of the men were supportive of their wives and even began to take interest in getting in shape themselves. Even with their very active agricultural work, 70.4% the men in the study were overweight or obese compared with 78% of the women. Many of the men had the attitude that since they worked hard all day, they did not need to exercise–off-season and weekends were considered times to relax. The complex factors that led to individuals gaining too much weight were embodied in discourses that index religion, immigration, poverty and a woman's duty to her family. Simply suggesting a low carbohydrate diet and a bit more aerobic exercise was futile, at best.

Sustos, Corajes and Bilis . . .

> The first thing I found waiting at home for me after my car accident was my mother with a *te amarga* (bitter tea). She gave it to me so that the *susto* from me wrecking my car wouldn't give me diabetes or any other health problem. (HHP promotora)

While many individuals in the first round of home-visits knew few specifics about diabetes, other than it was "bad," "it kills you" and "it is too much sugar in the blood," over 50% of the participants attributed diabetes to *corajes*, *sustos*, and *espantos* (angers and frights). The emotional upsets that individuals feel due to accidents, immigration status, problems with the legal system, poverty and other negative life-experiences were often encoded in their narratives about where their diabetes came from. The generative themes that engage individuals in talking about their diabetes are the narratives surrounding the *corajes* and *sustos* that are attributed to causing their diabetes. Other generative themes are women's discourses on the meaning of food for themselves and for their families, and the meanings of the social presentations of the body and how that is integrally linked to notions of humility and vanity. These are the themes that will be pursued in the Year Two interviews and discussed and analyzed via age, time in the U.S. and gender. While these themes may well be generalizable to many Hispanic farmworker communities, it is the process of engaging individuals in discussing what the "Latino Folk Illnesses" mean to them at a particular time that is important.

DISCUSSION

The results of the Formando project have demonstrated to community members enrolled in the project and to the HHP team a real need to engage in decreasing the effects of type 2 diabetes in the study communities. Individuals participating in the project now are beginning the process of understanding the relationship between their BMIs and increases in blood glucose levels. Indeed, many of the participants in Formando did not have scales in their homes; we will provide scales to the families in Year Two. The composite quantitative results are being shared with the community during both our health education programs and at community gatherings and health fairs.

The qualitative results indicate that we need to understand better the relationship between culturally acceptable notions of thinness, the meaning of foods and fullness, and how those issues are locally contextualized during social events and family meals. Another important finding was that individuals do not discuss type 2 diabetes within their families, even if family members have the disease. Addressing how type 2 diabetes is experienced by the whole family unit is essential; a lack of inter-personal communication about this disease within families is a real barrier to overcome in changing meal preparation and family physical activities. Both the stigma of diabetes and the lack of information play into this dynamic. The social themes that came out of the interviews show that health practitioners in the U.S. have a real opportunity to explore the lifeworld of Mexican agricultural workers and their families through engaging in a dialogue about why these individual think that they have their *sustos, corajes,* and *nervios.* It is important to recognize that although many individuals in the Hispanic culture attribute ultimate causation of an illness to these "Latino Folk Illnesses" they are also willing and able to understand the "biomedically-recognized" interactions between diabetes, diet, exercise and their ability to control the symptoms that are associated with type 2 diabetes.

CONCLUSIONS

Engaging Hispanic women farmworkers and their families in the *Formando* project has been somewhat successful because of the manner in which the past projects were conducted by the promotores and because the promotores come from the community and are ex-farmworkers themselves. Each year the women and their families can see and discuss the results of their biometric tests as well as engage in a more detailed discussion about the prevention and control of type 2 diabetes.

The study had several limitations. One was that the individuals who traveled to work in agriculture were under-represented in the total database. While our existing manner of recruiting has been effective in getting individuals into the Year One phase, it has been more difficult to contact those who do not have permanent houses in the area. While this is a small percentage (less than 10%) of the agricultural workforce, these are also some of the most recent immigrants from Mexico and are also mostly young men. Over 90% of the individuals in this study live in the area all year; thus, the results may not be representative of more mobile farmworker populations. All equipment for measuring heights and weights was checked periodically, but a small amount of error may have occurred from using the scales and stadiometer on different kinds of floors. The self-reported medical information may have also been reported incorrectly.

Brown and Vega's (1996) protocol for community based participatory research (CBPR) asks community members and researchers to question: how the research will serve the community, how the community will be involved, if the researchers are committed to following-up on their projects, how the community will be involved in the analysis of the data, how the research will affect perceptions of the community, how the findings will be released, how long term community needs will be addressed, and whether the research is rigorous enough to be a real reflection of the community as well as be acceptable by the scientific community at large. The work done at the HHP so far has demonstrated that the day-to-day negotiation and relationship building is the most fundamental part of being able to continue working in communities over time with the goal of advocating for the cause of the medically underserved. Research, when couched in terms of advocacy, moves at a different pace than research in other venues (e.g., Minkler & Wallerstein 2003). The recognition of the time it takes to establish real communication, especially with immigrant communities who are displaced and who speak different languages, should be acknowledged by federal funding agencies whose grant cycles are often one or two years in length. Flexibility within the research process that truly attends to giving the community some say in the direction of the research is imperative; that flexibility along with reliable health information will allow for individuals to identify the research themes that are most meaningful to them.

As for the HHP's work, identifying generative themes that would engage community members in action to become advocates for their own health, we still have much to do. Individuals who are participating in the aerobics classes and the healthy cooking classes are those who are interested in making behavioral changes significant enough to affect their health status. Others are willing to talk, to ask questions and to continue having the HHP promotores take their blood glucose levels, heights, weights and blood pressures. With the continued, sustained efforts of the HHP on this issue, other individuals may feel supported enough to change their eating or exercise habits. Change could also come from a totally different avenue–young adults getting better educations and jobs might facilitate different attitudes about eating and body image. Of course, this could be for the worse, too as in the case of increased consumption of fast food and less physical activity. Advocacy, when it is focused at the level of helping individuals to understand an issue and to begin to effect the needed changes in their own and their family's health, takes time and patience.

NOTES

1. The majority of the agricultural workers who are involved in our projects call themselves "Mexicans" although some also use "Hispanic" to describe themselves. The terms are used interchangeably here. Most of the individuals who have contact with the HHP have come to the U.S. in the last 10 years or so from Mexico to work in the potato, wheat and sugar beet fields of SE Idaho. Many also work in the potato processing factories for part of the year.

2. Hispanic Health Projects, Department of Anthropology, Idaho State University, Pocatello, Idaho 83209. The HHP is funded, in part, by grants at the Department of Anthropology and the Institute of Rural Health at Idaho State University. This project is supported in part by grant # 1 D1B TM 00042-01 from the Department of Health and Human Services (DHHS) Health Resources and Services Department of Health and Human Services (DHHS) Health Resources and Services Administration, Office for the Advancement of Telehealth. Additional funding comes from The Corporation for National and Community Service, AmeriCorps and Vista Program through the National Association of Community Health Centers in cooperation with the Idaho Primary Care Association, RYKA Women's Sports Foundation, Idaho Department of Health and Welfare, the Open Meadows foundation, National Science Foundation-Epscor, Rural Health Care Access Program, Health West, Inc., Montana Migrant Education, Rural Employment Opportunities of Montana, and the AVON breast cancer crusade. The contents are the sole responsibility of the authors and do not necessarily represent the official views of the funding agencies.

3. All research projects were reviewed and approved by the Human Subjects Committee, Idaho State University. Informed consents were written in both Spanish and English and were signed by all participants.

4. The Formando project was reviewed and approved by the Human Subjects Committee (institutional review board), Idaho State University. Informed consents were written in both Spanish and English and were signed by all participants.

5. "Ya, me chinge," "Now I am screwed" is a common expression among individuals that have been diagnosed with pre-diabetes and type 2 diabetes in this community. It implies that there is nothing more that can be done.

REFERENCES

American Diabetes Association (2002). Report of the Expert Committee on the Diagnosis and Classification of Diabetes Mellitus. *Diabetes Care 25*, S5-20.

Brown, L. & Vega, W.A. (1996). A Protocol for Community Based Research. *American Journal of Preventive Medicine 12*(4), 4-5.

Brown, S. et al. (2002). Culturally Competent Diabetes Self-Management Education for Mexican Americans. *Diabetes Care 25*(2), 259-268.

Cartwright, E. & Schaper, H. (2002). The Case of Diabetes Among Farmworkers in SE Idaho and Guanajuato, Mexico: Challenges in Binational Health Research. *Proceedings of the 2001-2002 Migrant Farmworker Stream Forums, U.S. Department of Health and Human Services, Bureau of Primary Health Care, August* 2002, 80-84.

Cartwright, E. & Schow, D. (2004). Why Salsa Aerobics Works. *Migrant Health Newsline, 21*(1), 2-3.

Cartwright, E., Schow, D., & Mitchell, D. (2004). The Promotora Model of Community-Based, Health Research and Intervention in a Binational Community in SE Idaho: Did We Say Salsa Aerobics Worked? *Anthropology News, 45*(5).

Durand, J., Massey, D., & Parrado, E. (1999). The New Era of Mexican Migration to the United States. *The Journal of American History, 86*(2), 518-536.

Early, J. (2000). Hispanic Farmworker Women and Depression in American Falls and Aberdeen. *Master's Thesis, Department of Anthropology, Idaho State University.*

Farmer, P. (2003). *Pathologies of Power: Health, Human Rights, and the New War on the Poor.* Berkeley, CA: University of California Press.

Ferzacca, S. (2000). Actually, I Don't Feel That Bad: Managing Diabetes and the Clinical Encounter. *Medical Anthropology Quarterly 14*(1), 28-50.

Fisher, E. B. et al. (2002). Behavioral Science Research in the Prevention of Diabetes: Status and Opportunities. *Diabetes Care 25*(3), 599-606.

Freire, P. (1970). *Pedagogy of the Oppressed.* New York: Continuum Press.

Guzzle, P. (2002), Explanatory Models of Sickness Used by Hispanic Male Farmworkers in Southeast Idaho: Follow-Up Interviews of the Healthy Families in Health Communities Project. *Master's Thesis, Department of Anthropology, Idaho State University.*

Heyman, J. M. (1995). Putting Power in the Anthropology of Bureaucracy: The Immigration and Naturalization Service at the Mexico-United States Border. *Current Anthropology 36*(2). 261-287.

Hunter, A.S., Cartwright, E., & Hall, T.R. (2001). Identifying Disparities in Health Service Utilization and Health Outcomes in Community Health Centers in SE Idaho. *Final Report for a Project funded by Idaho Health and Welfare Grant #HC27900.* 102 pp, MS.

Hunter, A., Hall, T., Hearn, G., & Cartwright, E. (2003). The Health Status of Hispanic Migrant Farmworkers in Idaho. *Texas Journal of Rural Health, 21*(1), 50-59.

Minkler, M. & N. Wallerstein, eds. (2003). *Community-Based Participatory Research for Health,* San Francisco: Jossey-Bass.

Neufeld et al. (1998). Early Presentation of Type 2 Diabetes in Mexican-American Youth. *Diabetes Care 21d*(1), 80-86.

Rice, P. L. & Ezzy, D. (1999). *Qualitative Research Methods: A Health Focus.* Melbourne: Oxford University Press.

Ryan, G.W. & Bernard, H.R. (2003). Techniques to Identify Themes. *Field Methods, 15*(1), 85-109.

Schoenberg, N. E., Ameyu, C. H., & Coward, R. T. (1998). Stories of Meaning: Lay Perspectives on the Origin and Management of Noninsulin Dependent Diabetes Mellitus

Among Older Women in the United States. *Social Science and Medicine 47*(12), 2113-2125.

Slesinger, D. (1992). Health Status and Needs of Migrant Farmworkers in the U.S.: A Literature Review. *The Journal of Rural Health, 8*(3), 227-233.

Stein H. (1985). *The Psychodynamics of Medical Practice: Unconscious Factors in Patient Care.* Berkeley: The University of California Press.

U.S. Census Bureau Statistics, 2000.

Villarejo, D. & Baron, S. (1999). The Occupational Health Status of Hired Farm Workers. *Occupational Medicine: State of the Art Reviews, 14*(3), 613-635.

Weller, S., Baer, R.D., Pachter, L.M., Trotter, R. T., Glazer, M., Garcia de Alba Garcia, J.E., & Klein, R. E. (1999). Latino Beliefs About Diabetes. *Diabetes Care, 22*(5), 722-728.

doi:10.1300/J013v43n04_06

Index

111

BOOK ORDER FORM!

Order a copy of this book with this form or online at:
http://www.HaworthPress.com/store/product.asp?sku= 5967

Women's Health
New Frontiers in Advocacy & Social Justice Research

—— in softbound at $14.00 ISBN-13: 978-0-7890-3331-4 / ISBN-10: 0-7890-3331-3.
—— in hardbound at $40.00 ISBN-13: 978-0-7890-3330-7 / ISBN-10: 0-7890-3330-5.

COST OF BOOKS _____

POSTAGE & HANDLING _____
US: $4.00 for first book & $1.50
for each additional book
Outside US: $5.00 for first book
& $2.00 for each additional book.

SUBTOTAL _____

In Canada: add 6% GST. _____

STATE TAX _____
CA, IL, IN, MN, NJ, NY, OH, PA & SD residents
please add appropriate local sales tax.

FINAL TOTAL _____

If paying in Canadian funds, convert
using the current exchange rate,
UNESCO coupons welcome.

❑ **BILL ME LATER:**
Bill-me option is good on US/Canada/
Mexico orders only; not good to jobbers,
wholesalers, or subscription agencies.

❑ **Signature** _____

❑ **Payment Enclosed: $**_____

❑ **PLEASE CHARGE TO MY CREDIT CARD:**

❑ Visa ❑ MasterCard ❑ AmEx ❑ Discover
❑ Diner's Club ❑ Eurocard ❑ JCB

Account #_____

Exp Date_____

Signature_____
(Prices in US dollars and subject to change without notice.)

PLEASE PRINT ALL INFORMATION OR ATTACH YOUR BUSINESS CARD

Name

Address

City   State/Province   Zip/Postal Code

Country

Tel   Fax

E-Mail

May we use your e-mail address for confirmations and other types of information? ❑Yes ❑No We appreciate receiving
your e-mail address. Haworth would like to e-mail special discount offers to you, as a preferred customer.
We will never share, rent, or exchange your e-mail address. We regard such actions as an invasion of your privacy.

Order from your **local bookstore** or directly from
The Haworth Press, Inc. 10 Alice Street, Binghamton, New York 13904-1580 • USA
Call our toll-free number (1-800-429-6784) / Outside US/Canada: (607) 722-5857
Fax: 1-800-895-0582 / Outside US/Canada: (607) 771-0012
E-mail your order to us: orders@HaworthPress.com

For orders outside US and Canada, you may wish to order through your local
sales representative, distributor, or bookseller.
For information, see http://HaworthPress.com/distributors

(Discounts are available for individual orders in US and Canada only, not booksellers/distributors.)

Please photocopy this form for your personal use.
www.HaworthPress.com

BOF06